# WHITEOUT

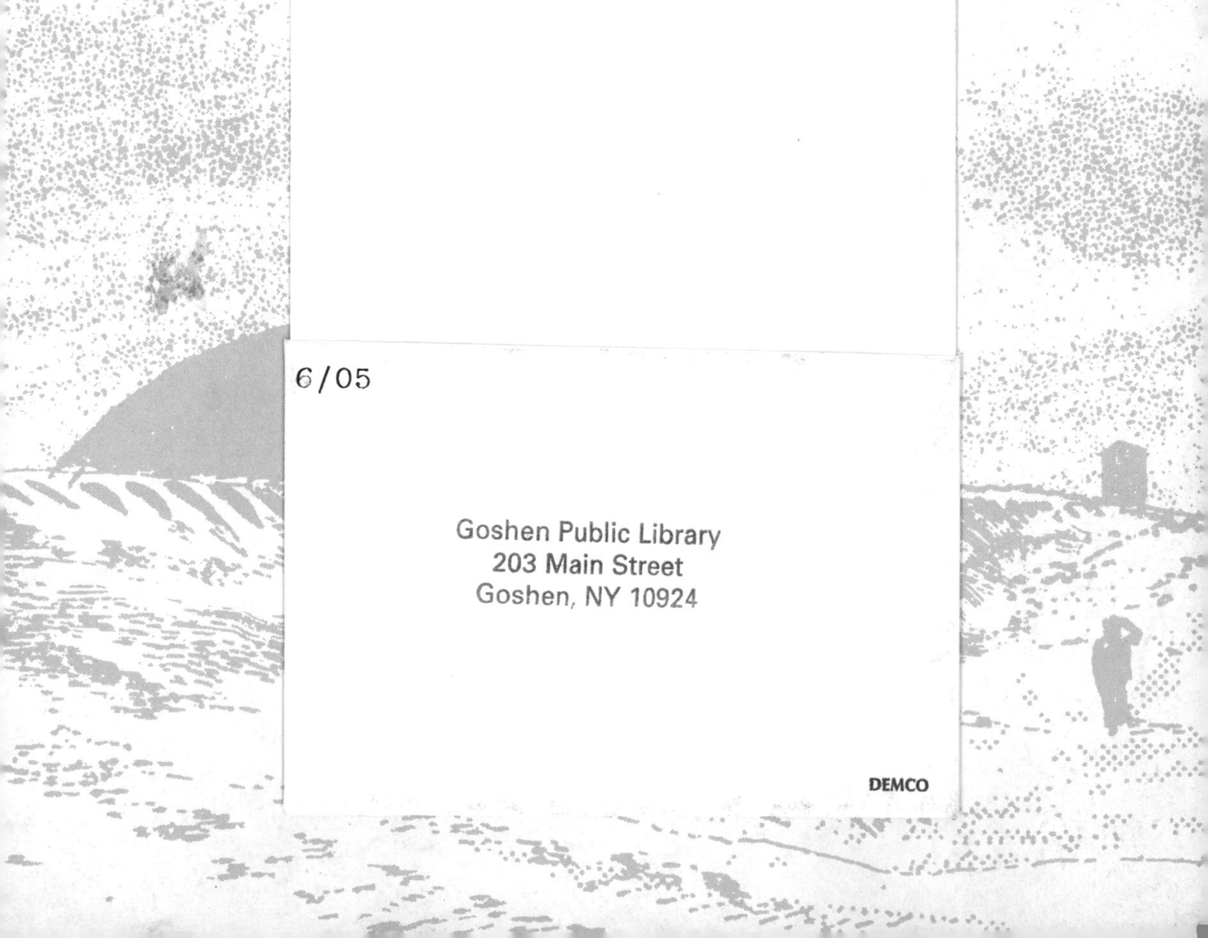

# WHITEOUT™

Created and written by

GREG RUCKA

Illustrated and lettered by

STEVE LIEBER



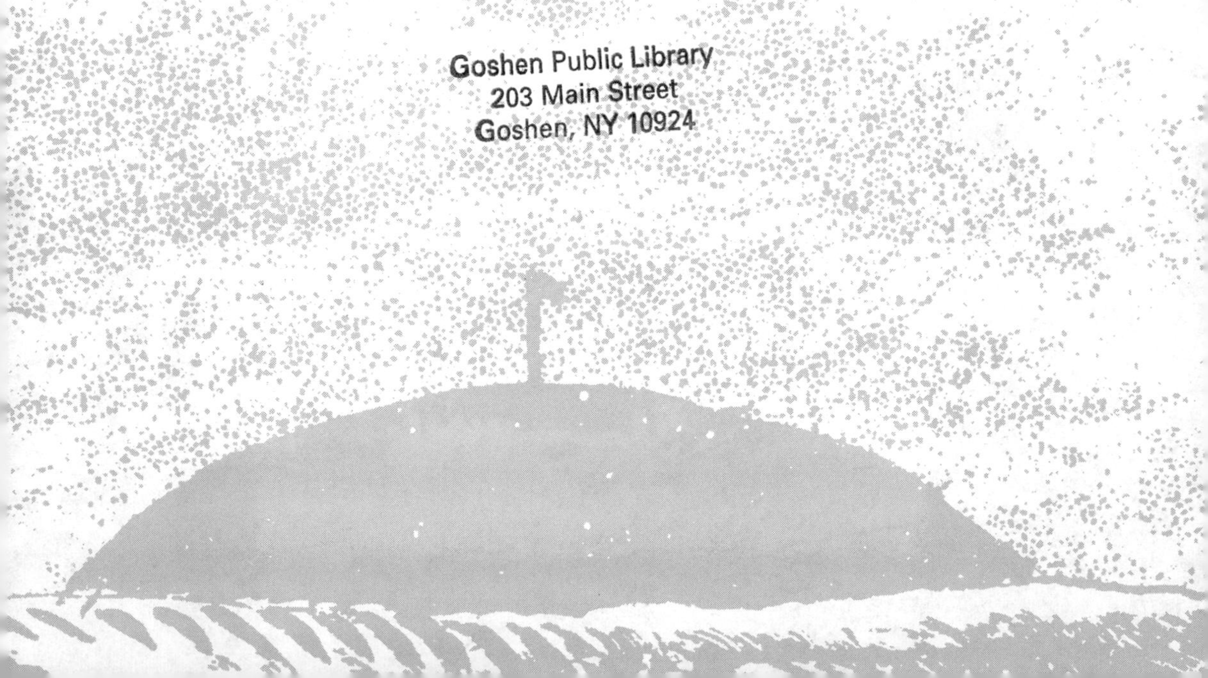

Cover art by
**FRANK MILLER**

Chapter art by
**MATT WAGNER**
**MIKE MIGNOLA**
**DAVE GIBBONS**
**STEVE LIEBER**

Cover logo by
**MONTY SHELDON**

Book design by
**STEVEN BIRCH AT SERVO**

Collection edited by
**JAMIE S. RICH**

Original series edited by
**BOB SCHRECK**
with
**JAMIE S. RICH**

Published by Oni Press, Inc.
BOB SCHRECK & JOE NOZEMACK, PUBLISHERS

This collects issues 1-4 of the Oni Press comic book *Whiteout*.

ONI PRESS, INC.
6336 SE Milwaukie Avenue, Suite 30
Portland, OR 97202
USA

www.onipress.com

First edition: May 1999
ISBN 0-9667127-1-4

5 7 9 10 8 6
PRINTED IN CANADA.

# CHAPTER
# ONE

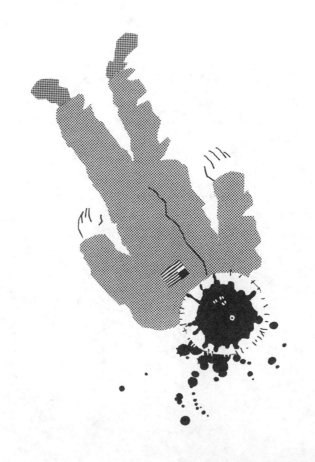

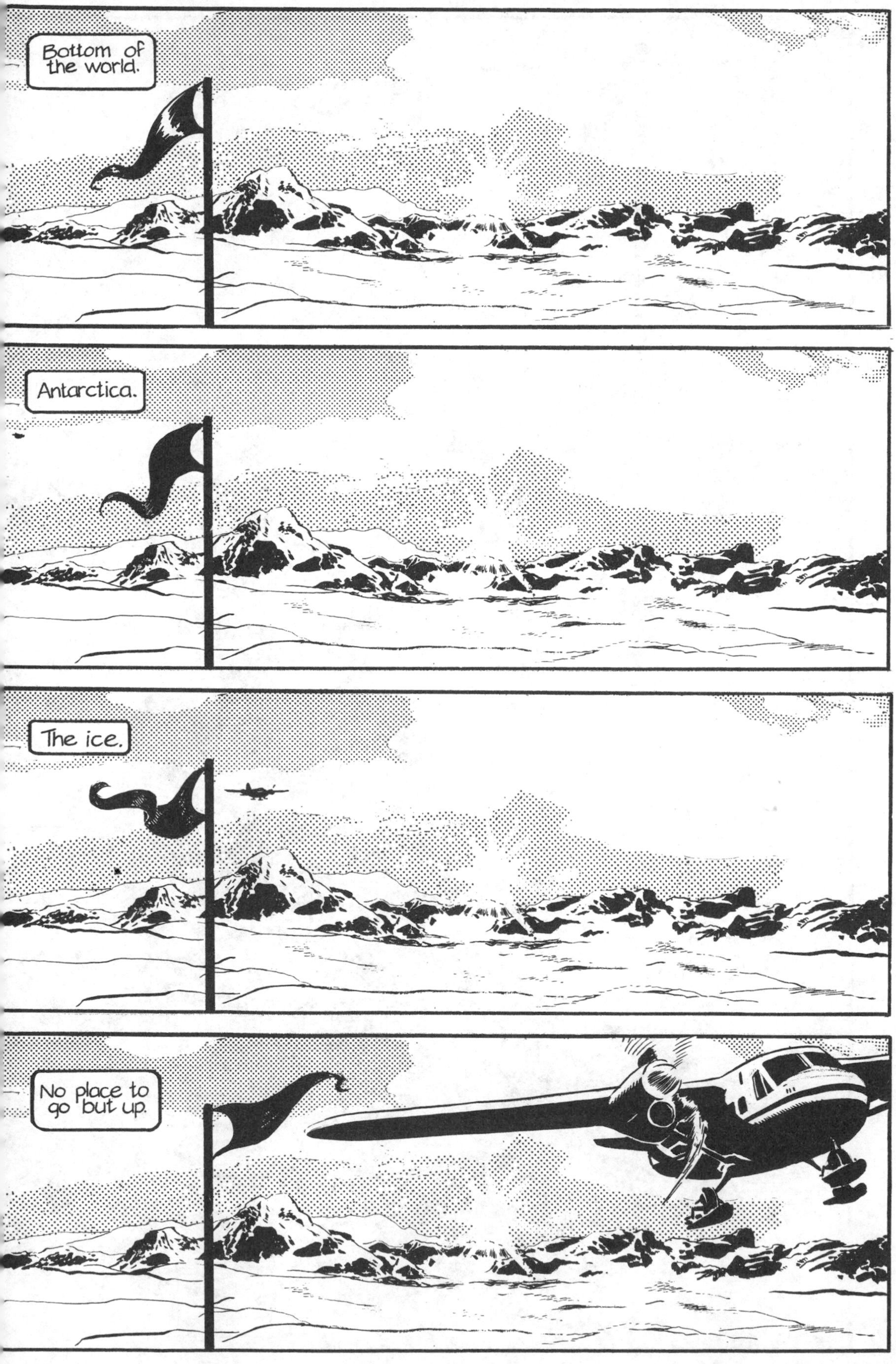
Bottom of the world.
Antarctica.
The ice.
No place to go but up.

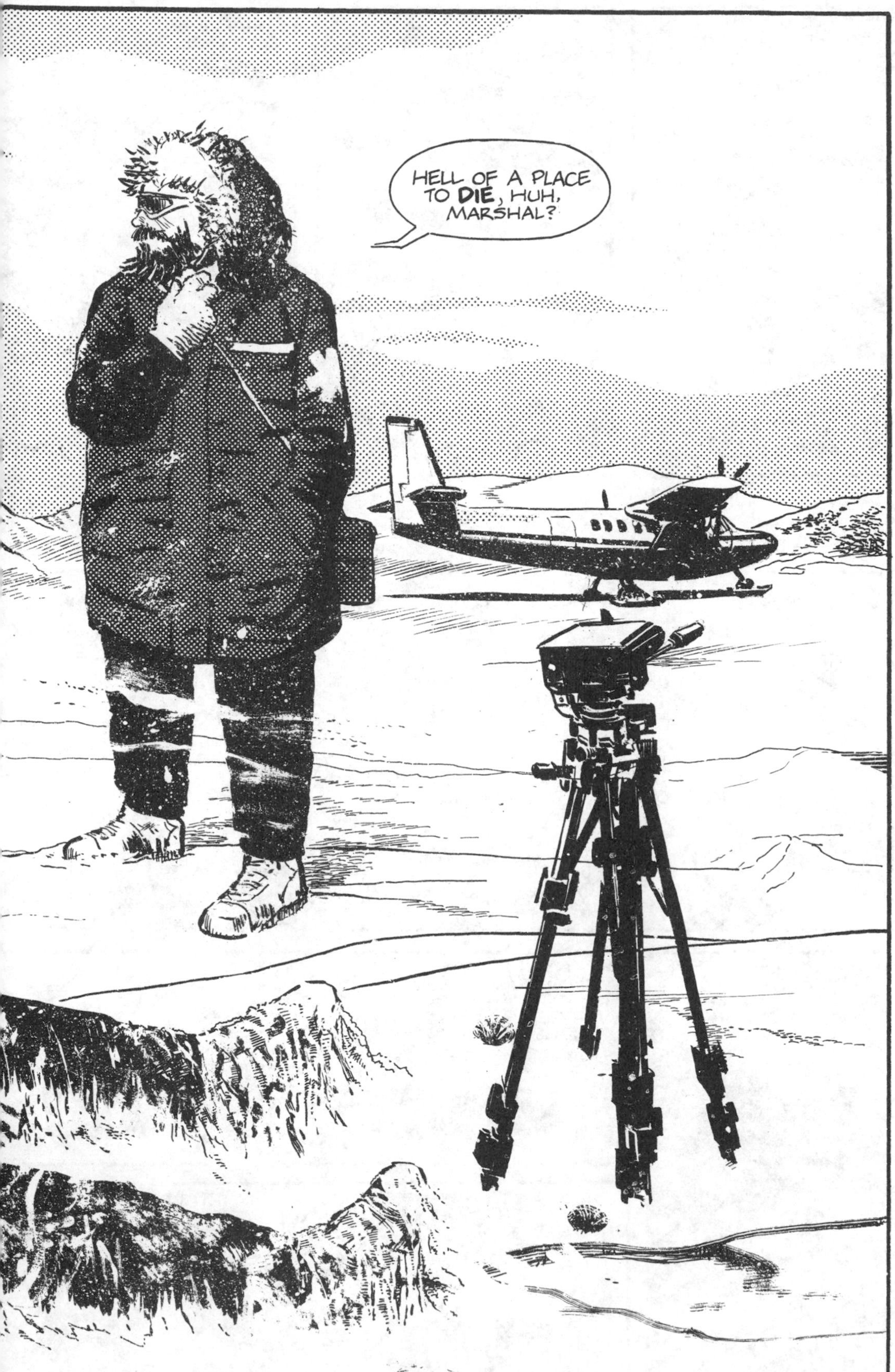
HELL OF A PLACE TO DIE, HUH, MARSHAL?

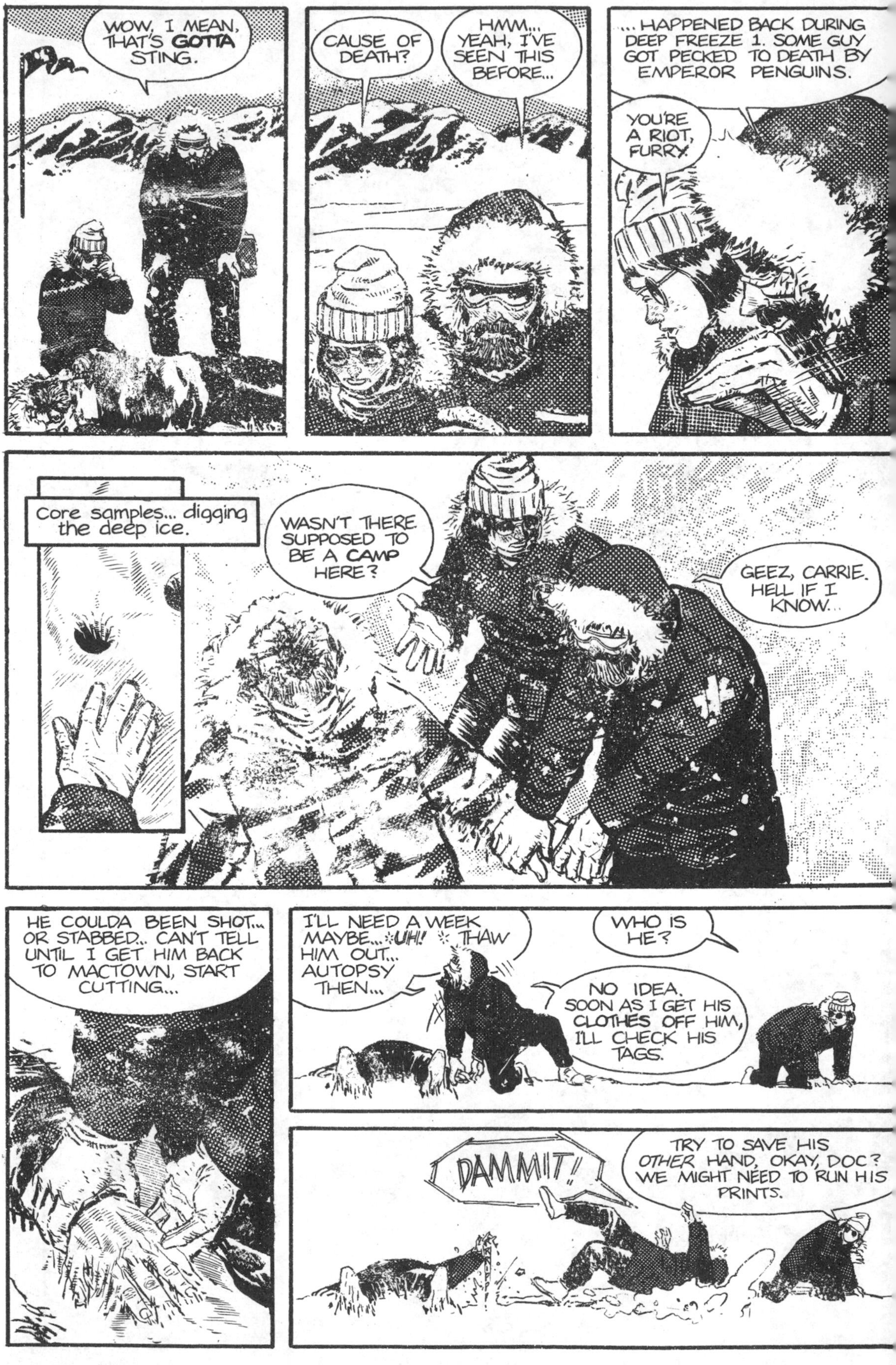

WOW, I MEAN, THAT'S GOTTA STING.
CAUSE OF DEATH?
HMM... YEAH, I'VE SEEN THIS BEFORE...
...HAPPENED BACK DURING DEEP FREEZE 1. SOME GUY GOT PECKED TO DEATH BY EMPEROR PENGUINS.
YOU'RE A RIOT, FURRY.
Core samples... digging the deep ice.
WASN'T THERE SUPPOSED TO BE A CAMP HERE?
GEEZ, CARRIE. HELL IF I KNOW...
HE COULDA BEEN SHOT... OR STABBED... CAN'T TELL UNTIL I GET HIM BACK TO MACTOWN, START CUTTING...
I'LL NEED A WEEK MAYBE... UH! THAW HIM OUT... AUTOPSY THEN...
WHO IS HE?
NO IDEA. SOON AS I GET HIS CLOTHES OFF HIM, I'LL CHECK HIS TAGS.
DAMMIT!
TRY TO SAVE HIS OTHER HAND, OKAY, DOC? WE MIGHT NEED TO RUN HIS PRINTS.

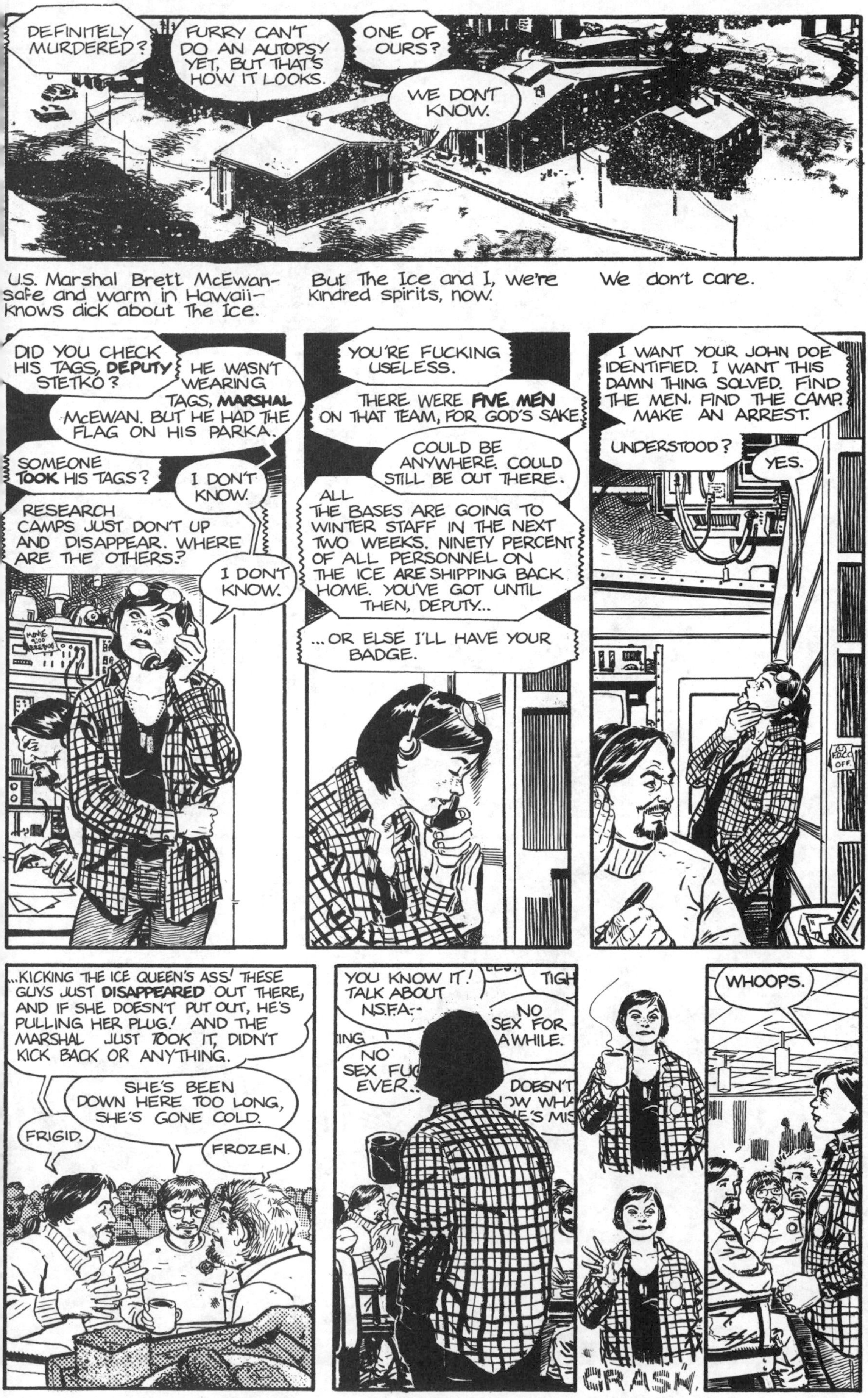
DEFINITELY MURDERED?
FURRY CAN'T DO AN AUTOPSY YET, BUT THAT'S HOW IT LOOKS.
ONE OF OURS?
WE DON'T KNOW.
U.S. Marshal Brett McEwan- safe and warm in Hawaii- knows dick about The Ice.
But The Ice and I, we're kindred spirits, now.
We don't care.
DID YOU CHECK HIS TAGS, DEPUTY STETKO?
HE WASN'T WEARING TAGS, MARSHAL McEWAN. BUT HE HAD THE FLAG ON HIS PARKA.
SOMEONE TOOK HIS TAGS?
I DON'T KNOW.
RESEARCH CAMPS JUST DON'T UP AND DISAPPEAR. WHERE ARE THE OTHERS?
I DON'T KNOW.
YOU'RE FUCKING USELESS.
THERE WERE FIVE MEN ON THAT TEAM, FOR GOD'S SAKE.
COULD BE ANYWHERE. COULD STILL BE OUT THERE.
ALL THE BASES ARE GOING TO WINTER STAFF IN THE NEXT TWO WEEKS. NINETY PERCENT OF ALL PERSONNEL ON THE ICE ARE SHIPPING BACK HOME. YOU'VE GOT UNTIL THEN, DEPUTY...
...OR ELSE I'LL HAVE YOUR BADGE.
I WANT YOUR JOHN DOE IDENTIFIED. I WANT THIS DAMN THING SOLVED. FIND THE MEN. FIND THE CAMP. MAKE AN ARREST.
UNDERSTOOD?
YES.
...KICKING THE ICE QUEEN'S ASS! THESE GUYS JUST DISAPPEARED OUT THERE, AND IF SHE DOESN'T PUT OUT, HE'S PULLING HER PLUG! AND THE MARSHAL JUST TOOK IT, DIDN'T KICK BACK OR ANYTHING.
SHE'S BEEN DOWN HERE TOO LONG, SHE'S GONE COLD.
FRIGID.
FROZEN.
YOU KNOW IT! TALK ABOUT N.S.F.A.-
NO SEX FOR AWHILE.
NO SEX FUC EVER..
DOESN'T
WHOOPS.
CRASH.

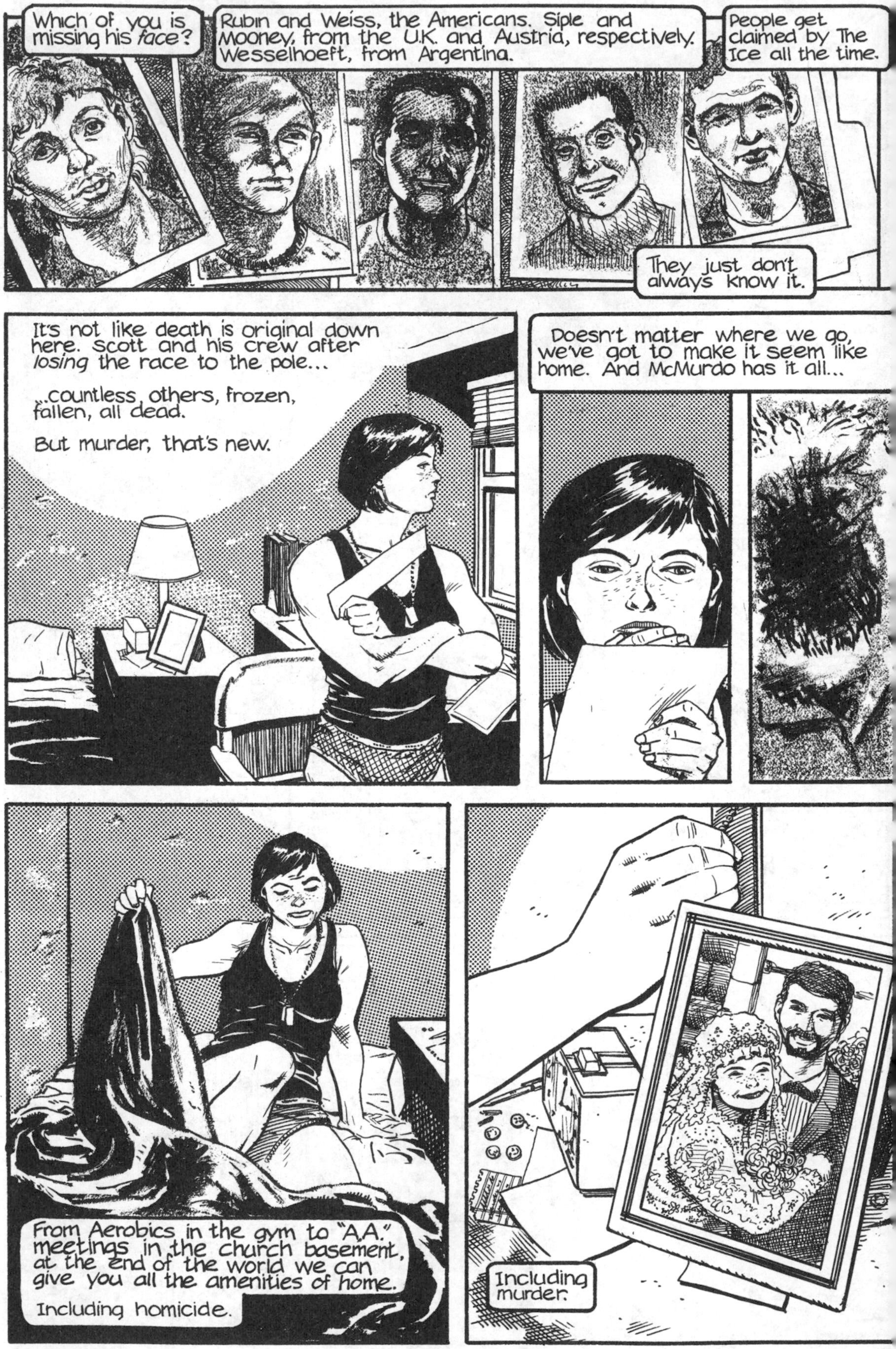
Which of you is missing his *face*?
Rubin and Weiss, the Americans. Siple and Mooney, from the U.K. and Austria, respectively. Wesselhoeft, from Argentina.
People get claimed by The Ice all the time.
They just don't always know it.
It's not like death is original down here. Scott and his crew after *losing* the race to the pole...
...countless others, frozen, fallen, all dead.
But murder, that's new.
Doesn't matter where we go, we've got to make it seem like home. And McMurdo has it all...
From Aerobics in the gym to "A.A." meetings in the church basement, at the end of the world we can give you all the amenities of home.
Including homicide.
Including murder.

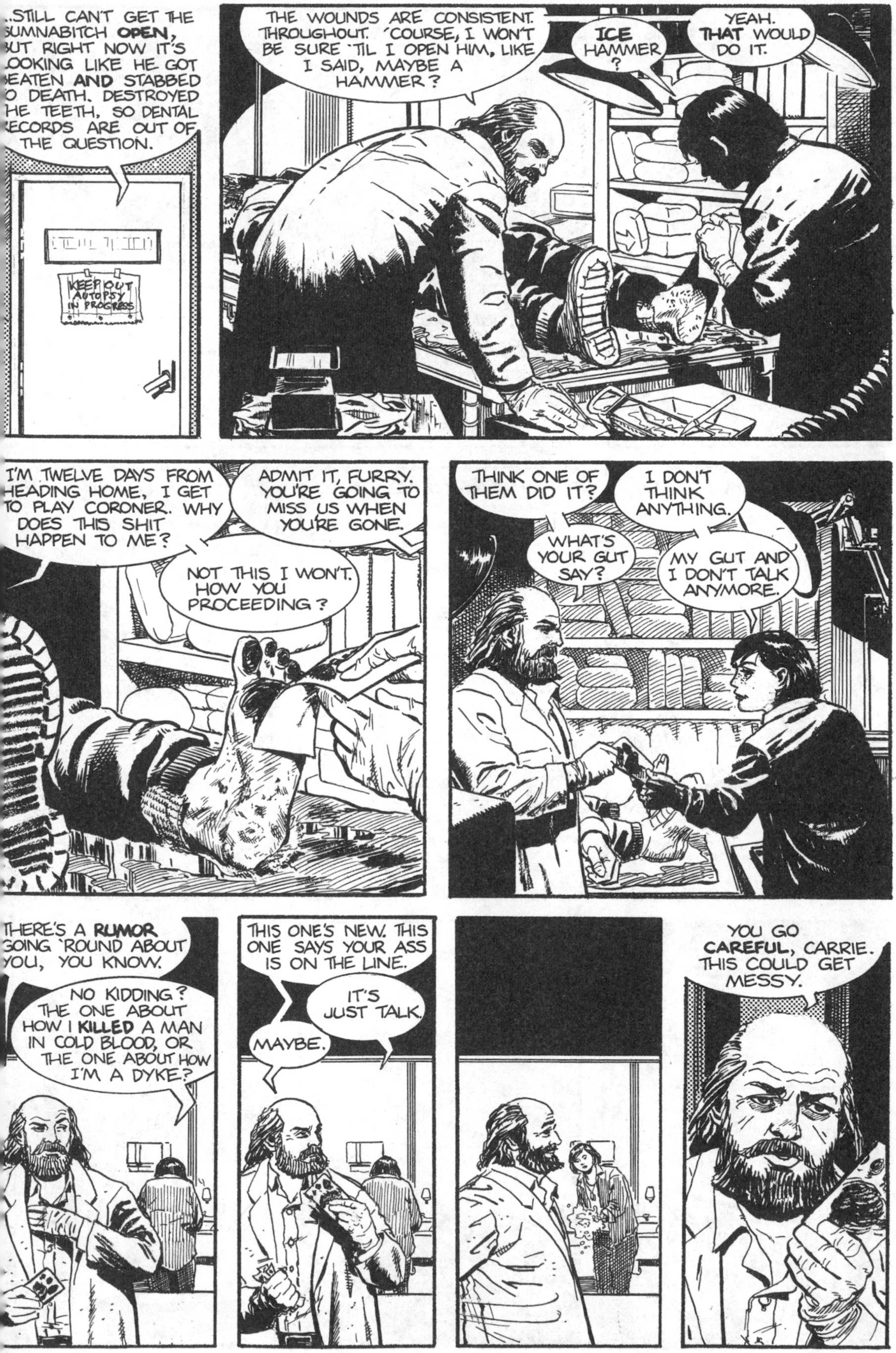
..STILL CAN'T GET THE SUMNABITCH OPEN, BUT RIGHT NOW IT'S LOOKING LIKE HE GOT BEATEN AND STABBED TO DEATH. DESTROYED THE TEETH, SO DENTAL RECORDS ARE OUT OF THE QUESTION.
KEEP OUT AUTOPSY IN PROGRESS
THE WOUNDS ARE CONSISTENT. THROUGHOUT. 'COURSE, I WON'T BE SURE 'TIL I OPEN HIM, LIKE I SAID, MAYBE A HAMMER?
ICE HAMMER?
YEAH. THAT WOULD DO IT.
I'M TWELVE DAYS FROM HEADING HOME, I GET TO PLAY CORONER. WHY DOES THIS SHIT HAPPEN TO ME?
ADMIT IT, FURRY. YOU'RE GOING TO MISS US WHEN YOU'RE GONE.
NOT THIS I WON'T. HOW YOU PROCEEDING?
THINK ONE OF THEM DID IT?
I DON'T THINK ANYTHING.
WHAT'S YOUR GUT SAY?
MY GUT AND I DON'T TALK ANYMORE.
THERE'S A RUMOR GOING 'ROUND ABOUT YOU, YOU KNOW.
NO KIDDING? THE ONE ABOUT HOW I KILLED A MAN IN COLD BLOOD, OR THE ONE ABOUT HOW I'M A DYKE?
THIS ONE'S NEW. THIS ONE SAYS YOUR ASS IS ON THE LINE.
IT'S JUST TALK.
MAYBE.
YOU GO CAREFUL, CARRIE. THIS COULD GET MESSY.

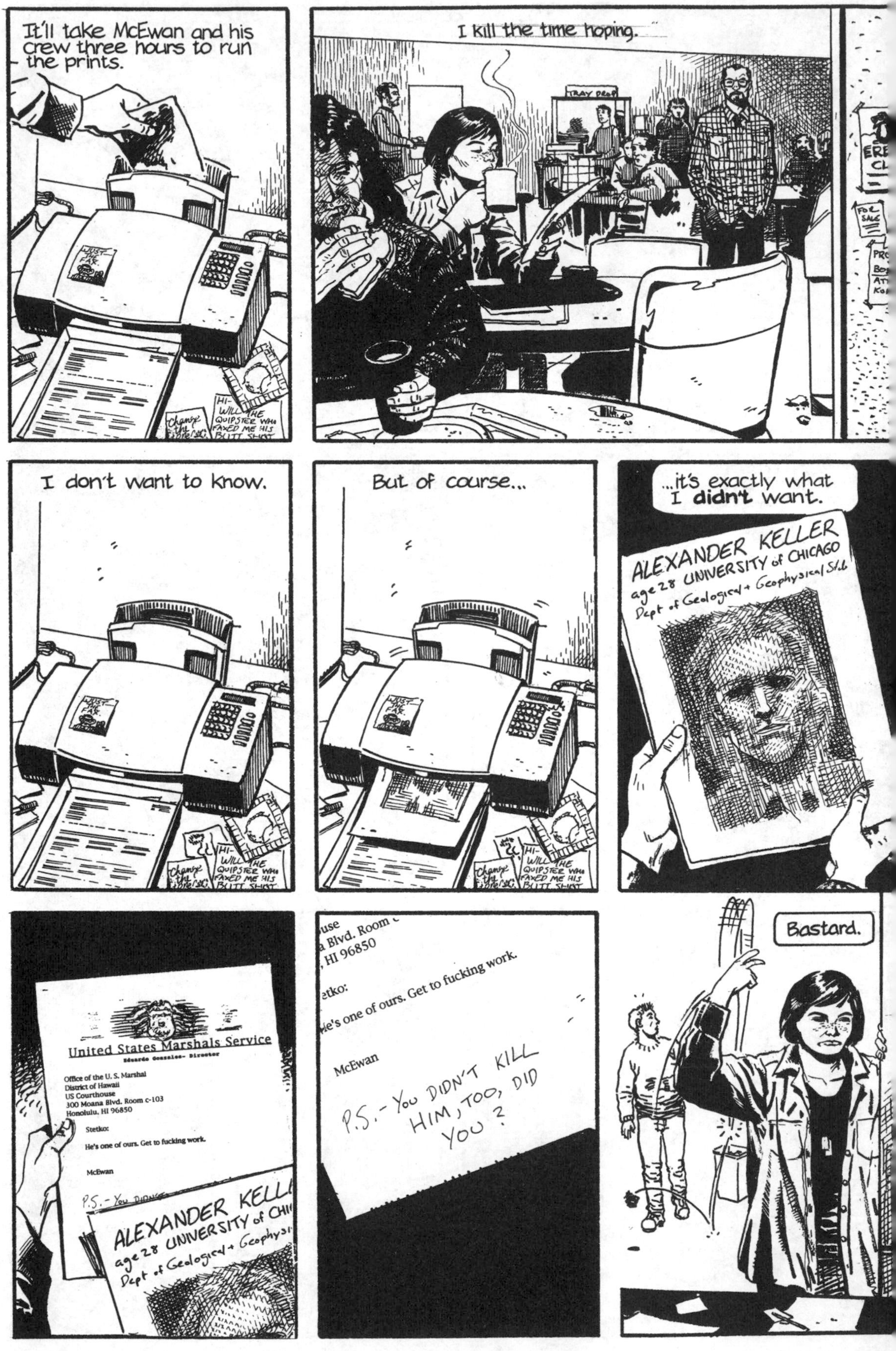

It'll take McEwan and his crew three hours to run the prints.
JUST THE FAX.
HI- WILL THE QUIPSTER WHO FAXED ME HIS BUTT SHOT
I kill the time hoping...
TRAY DROP
FOR SALE
I don't want to know.
But of course...
...it's exactly what I **didn't** want.
ALEXANDER KELLER
age 28 UNIVERSITY of CHICAGO
Dept of Geological + Geophysical Stud
United States Marshals Service
Eduardo Gonzales- Director
Office of the U. S. Marshal
District of Hawaii
US Courthouse
300 Moana Blvd. Room c-103
Honolulu, HI 96850
Stetko:
He's one of ours. Get to fucking work.
McEwan
McEwan
P.S. - You DIDN'T KILL HIM, TOO, DID YOU ?
Bastard.

McMurdo Station, MacTown. **McMudhole.**

YOURS IS THE RED ONE.

Named after McMurdo Sound, in turn named after Lt. Archibald McMurdo of HMS *Terror* way back in 1841.

McMurdo is the largest base on the Ice, with a summer head-count of over 1200, though in the next three weeks that number will fall to about 200. Even on the coast people don't like to stick around for the dark months.

The personnel is split three ways. The beakers, down here for research, spending their grant money. The support staff—custodians, cooks, mechanics. And the navy, or more precisely, those members of the Naval Support Force Antarctica. The N.S.F.A.

NOT FROM CONCENTRATE

DON'T DRINK THIS!

MCRDO NEEDS WOMEN

No Sex For A while.

Guy I'm looking for, he's an N.S.F.A. pilot, Lt. Byron Delfy...

He's the closest thing to a suspect I've got.

I **hate** churches.

LOO? YOU IN HERE?

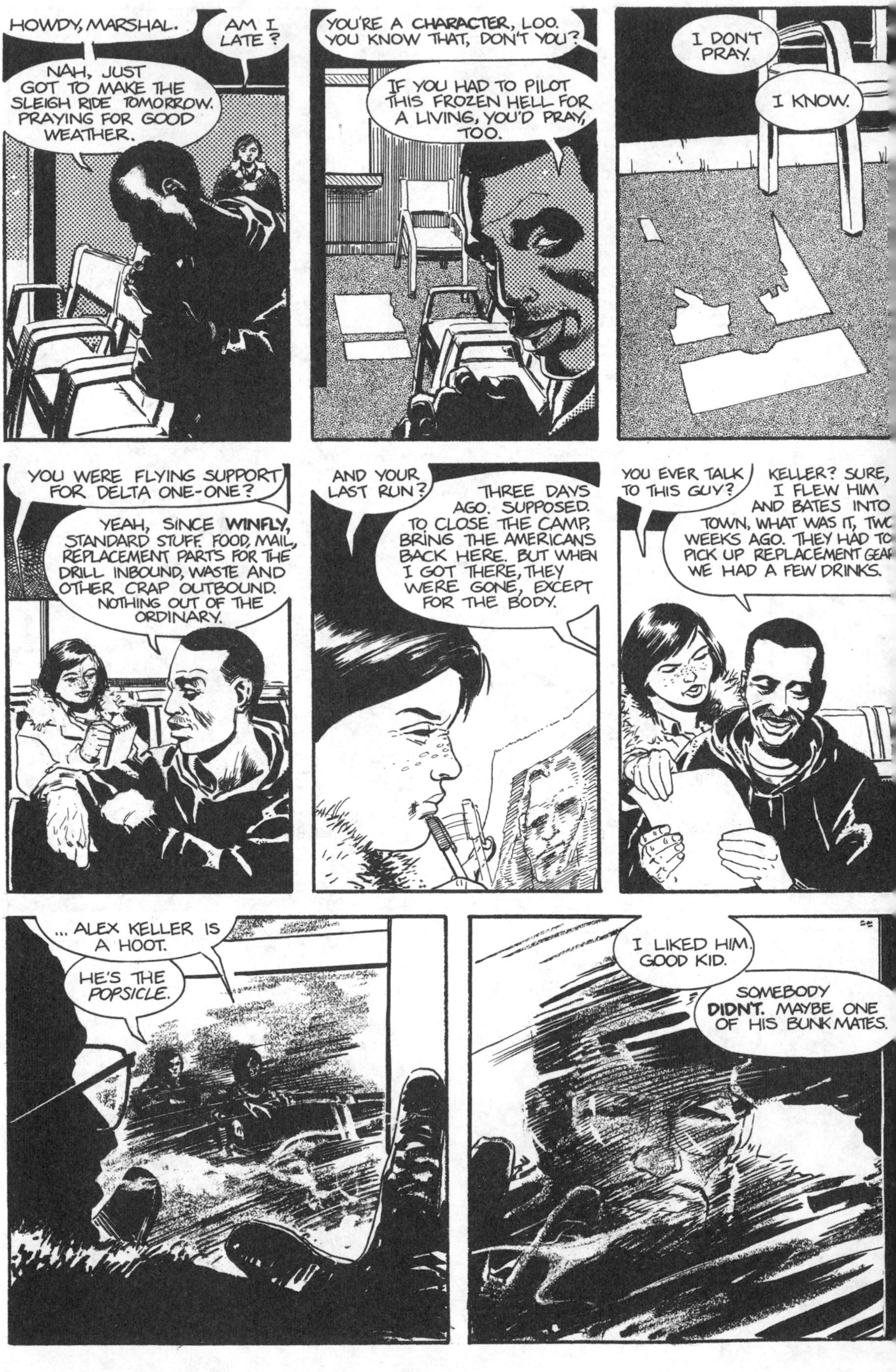
HOWDY, MARSHAL.
AM I LATE?
NAH, JUST GOT TO MAKE THE SLEIGH RIDE TOMORROW. PRAYING FOR GOOD WEATHER.
YOU'RE A CHARACTER, LOO. YOU KNOW THAT, DON'T YOU?
IF YOU HAD TO PILOT THIS FROZEN HELL FOR A LIVING, YOU'D PRAY, TOO.
I DON'T PRAY.
I KNOW.
YOU WERE FLYING SUPPORT FOR DELTA ONE-ONE?
YEAH, SINCE WINFLY. STANDARD STUFF. FOOD, MAIL, REPLACEMENT PARTS FOR THE DRILL INBOUND, WASTE AND OTHER CRAP OUTBOUND. NOTHING OUT OF THE ORDINARY.
AND YOUR LAST RUN?
THREE DAYS AGO. SUPPOSED TO CLOSE THE CAMP, BRING THE AMERICANS BACK HERE. BUT WHEN I GOT THERE, THEY WERE GONE, EXCEPT FOR THE BODY.
YOU EVER TALK TO THIS GUY?
KELLER? SURE, I FLEW HIM AND BATES INTO TOWN, WHAT WAS IT, TW WEEKS AGO. THEY HAD T PICK UP REPLACEMENT GEA WE HAD A FEW DRINKS.
... ALEX KELLER IS A HOOT.
HE'S THE POPSICLE.
I LIKED HIM. GOOD KID.
SOMEBODY DIDN'T. MAYBE ONE OF HIS BUNKMATES.

YOU SHOULD TALK TO THEM.

I DON'T KNOW WHERE **THEY** ARE. ANY IDEAS?

CHECK THE BASES. THEY WERE CLOSING THE CAMP FOR THE WINTER. I EXPECT EVERYONE WAS HEADING HOME.

THEY HAD TO BE **FLOWN** OUT OF THERE SOMEHOW.

YOU'RE NOT ACCUSING **ME** OF ANYTHING, ARE YOU, MARSHAL?

WHY? ARE YOU GUILTY OF SOMETHING?

THEY DIDN'T **WALK** OUT OF THERE, LOO. SOMEONE GAVE THEM A **LIFT.**

WASN'T ME.

THEN WHO?

I'LL ASK AROUND.

I'D APPRECIATE THAT.

BUY YOU SOME CHEER?

YOU BUY IT, I'LL DRINK IT.

DELFY, YOU'RE A MOOCH.

MAN, HADEN, WHERE'VE YOU BEEN, YOU POME FUCK?

MAWSON, FLYING FOR MY PEOPLE, YA YANKEE FAGGOT!

...WAS THAT THE MARSHAL I SAW YOU TALKING WITH EARLIER?

I spend the next **two days** on the radio trying to find my missing men.

Waiting for a call back from someone, **anyone**, who knows what I'm talking about.

I get fucking nowhere.

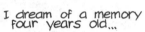

I dream of a memory four years old...

I don't like how it makes me **feel**...

The ratio of men to women on The Ice is something like **200** to **1**. That's during the **summer**. During **winter** it's more like **400** to **1**.

This causes many of the men to forget their manners.

DON'T DO THAT.

...YOU'VE GOT A CALL.

If they had any manners to forget.

IT'S NOT McEWAN, IS IT?

IT'S VICTORIA.

STETKO. GO AHEAD.

AH, MARSHAL, HALLO, HOW'S YOUR WEATHER?

HAVEN'T BEEN OUTSIDE. IS THIS GRANT?

INDEED. YOU CALLED ABOUT TWO OF OUR PEOPLE, CORRECT? SIPLE AND **MOONEY**?

THEY'RE HERE, BUT NOT FOR LONG. TAKING TOMORROW'S FLIGHT BACK TO THE WORLD.

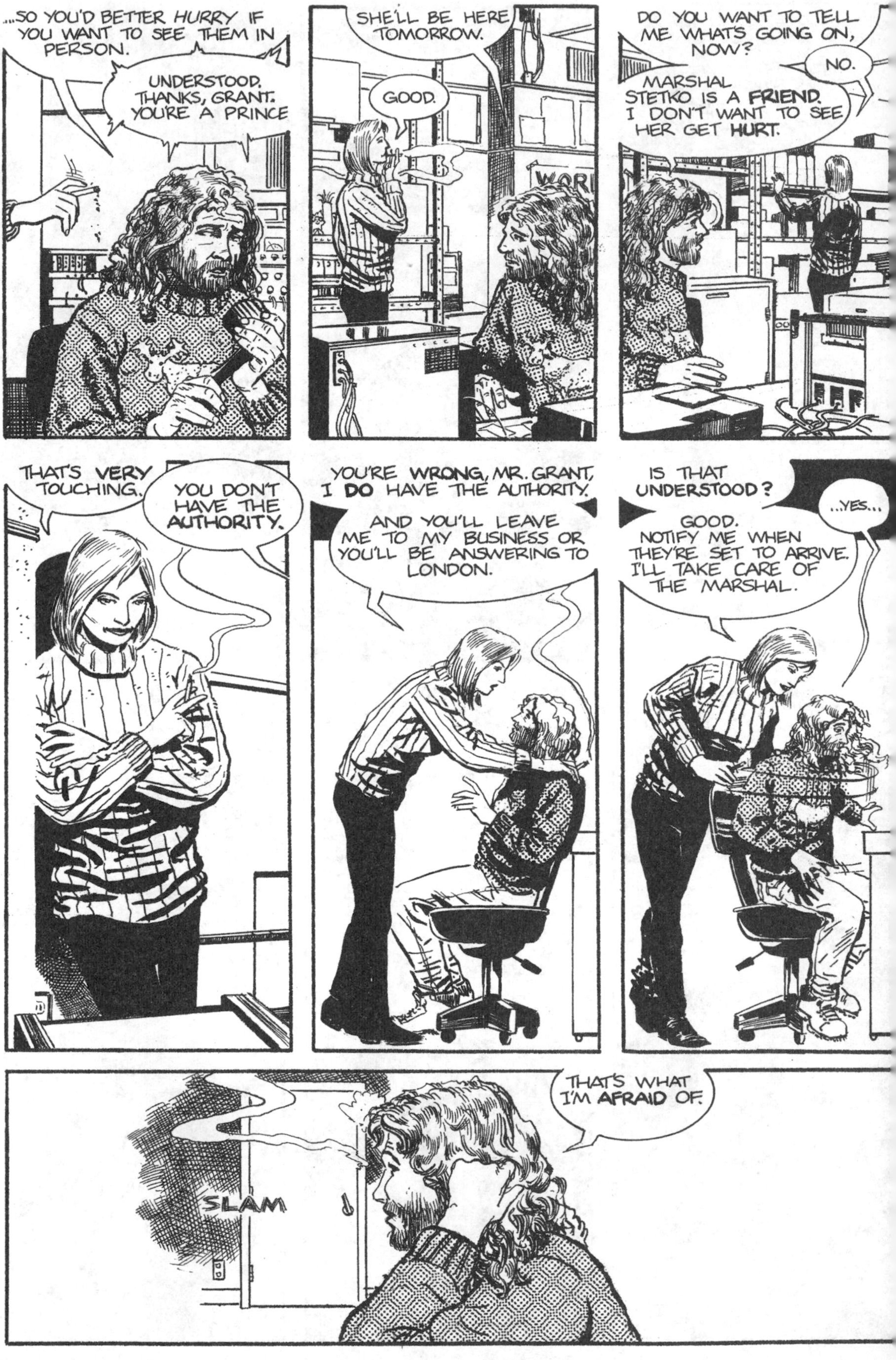

...SO YOU'D BETTER *HURRY* IF YOU WANT TO SEE THEM IN PERSON.
UNDERSTOOD. THANKS, GRANT. YOU'RE A PRINCE
SHE'LL BE HERE TOMORROW.
GOOD.
DO YOU WANT TO TELL ME WHAT'S GOING ON, NOW?
NO.
MARSHAL STETKO IS A **FRIEND**. I DON'T WANT TO SEE HER GET **HURT**.
THAT'S **VERY** TOUCHING.
YOU DON'T HAVE THE **AUTHORITY**.
YOU'RE **WRONG**, MR. GRANT, I **DO** HAVE THE AUTHORITY.
AND YOU'LL LEAVE ME TO MY BUSINESS OR YOU'LL BE ANSWERING TO LONDON.
IS THAT **UNDERSTOOD**?
...YES...
GOOD. NOTIFY ME WHEN THEY'RE SET TO ARRIVE. I'LL TAKE CARE OF THE MARSHAL.
SLAM
THAT'S WHAT I'M **AFRAID** OF.

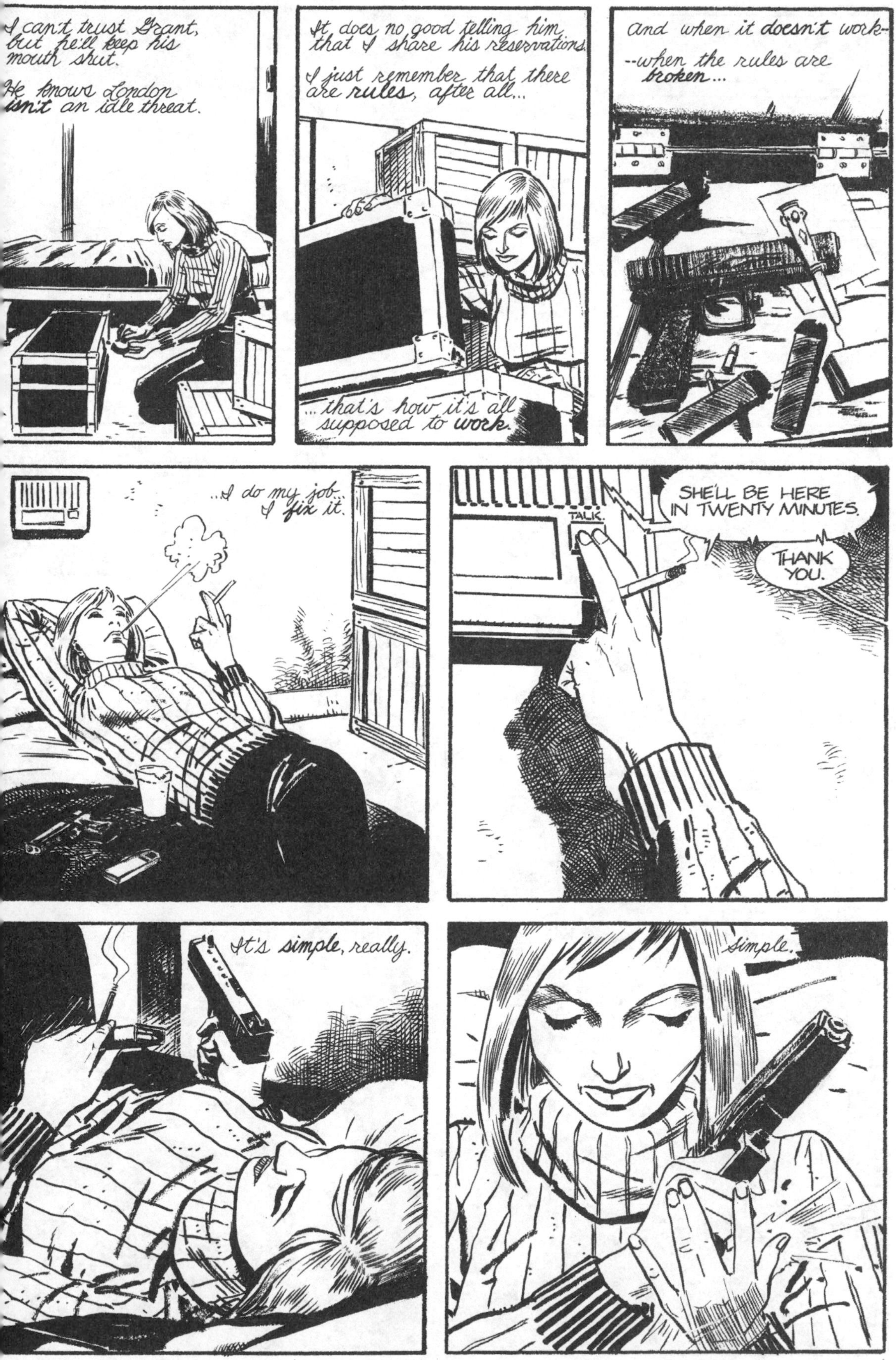
I can't trust Grant, but he'll keep his mouth shut.
He knows London isn't an idle threat.
It does no good telling him that I share his reservations.
I just remember that there are rules, after all...
...that's how it's all supposed to work.
And when it doesn't work--
--when the rules are broken...
...I do my job. I fix it.
TALK
SHE'LL BE HERE IN TWENTY MINUTES.
THANK YOU.
It's simple, really.
Simple.

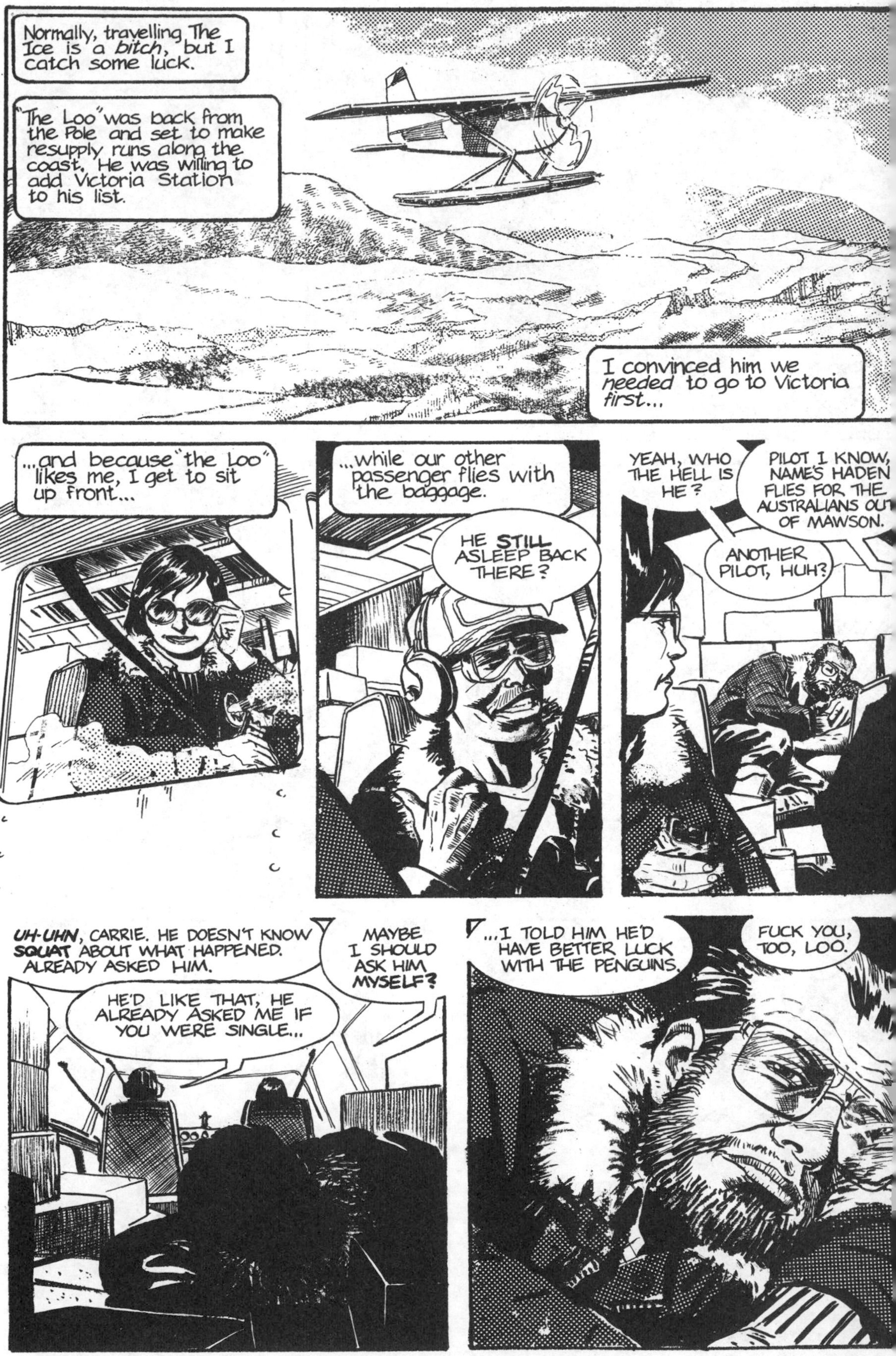
Normally, travelling The Ice is a *bitch*, but I catch some luck.
"The Loo" was back from the Pole and set to make resupply runs along the coast. He was willing to add Victoria Station to his list.
I convinced him we *needed* to go to Victoria *first*...
...and because "the Loo" likes me, I get to sit up front...
...while our other passenger flies with the baggage.
HE **STILL** ASLEEP BACK THERE?
YEAH, WHO THE HELL IS HE?
PILOT I KNOW, NAME'S HADEN FLIES FOR THE AUSTRALIANS OUT OF MAWSON.
ANOTHER PILOT, HUH?
**UH-UHN**, CARRIE. HE DOESN'T KNOW **SQUAT** ABOUT WHAT HAPPENED. ALREADY ASKED HIM.
MAYBE I SHOULD ASK HIM **MYSELF?**
HE'D LIKE THAT, HE ALREADY ASKED ME IF YOU WERE SINGLE...
...I TOLD HIM HE'D HAVE BETTER LUCK WITH THE PENGUINS.
FUCK YOU, TOO, LOO.

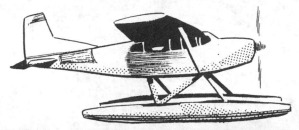

VICTORIA UK, THIS IS CHARLIE HOTEL EIGHT-NINER OUT OF McMURDO. HOW'S YOUR WEATHER? OVER.

...WIND AT SEVEN KNOTS FROM SSE... GOOD LANDING CONDITIONS BUT BE ADVISED...

...SITUATION UNSTABLE... WINDS FORECAST TO REACH 60 PLUS KNOTS IN NEXT FOUR HOURS. OVER.

ROGER THAT, VICTORIA...

...WE'RE ON FINAL APPROACH NOW.

BE ADVISED THAT HER MAJESTY'S GOVERNMENT CANNOT GRANT PERMISSION FOR LANDING OR ASSISTANCE DURING YOUR STAY, AND THAT YOU VISIT VICTORIA STATION AT YOUR OWN RISK. OVER.

CONFIRMED. OVER AND OUT.

DON'T YOU LOVE IT WHEN THEY COVER THEIR ASSES LIKE THAT? WHAT THEY'RE REALLY SAYING IS, IF YOU GET YOUR TITS IN THE WRINGER, YOU'RE ON YOUR OWN."

YOU HAVE SUCH A WAY WITH WORDS, HADEN.

WE COULD HAVE A PROBLEM, THOUGH...

...THE WINDS KICK UP, WE'LL BE GROUNDED, GOD KNOWS FOR HOW LONG.

...NOT THAT YOU'D MIND.

SORRY, WHAT?

NOTHING.

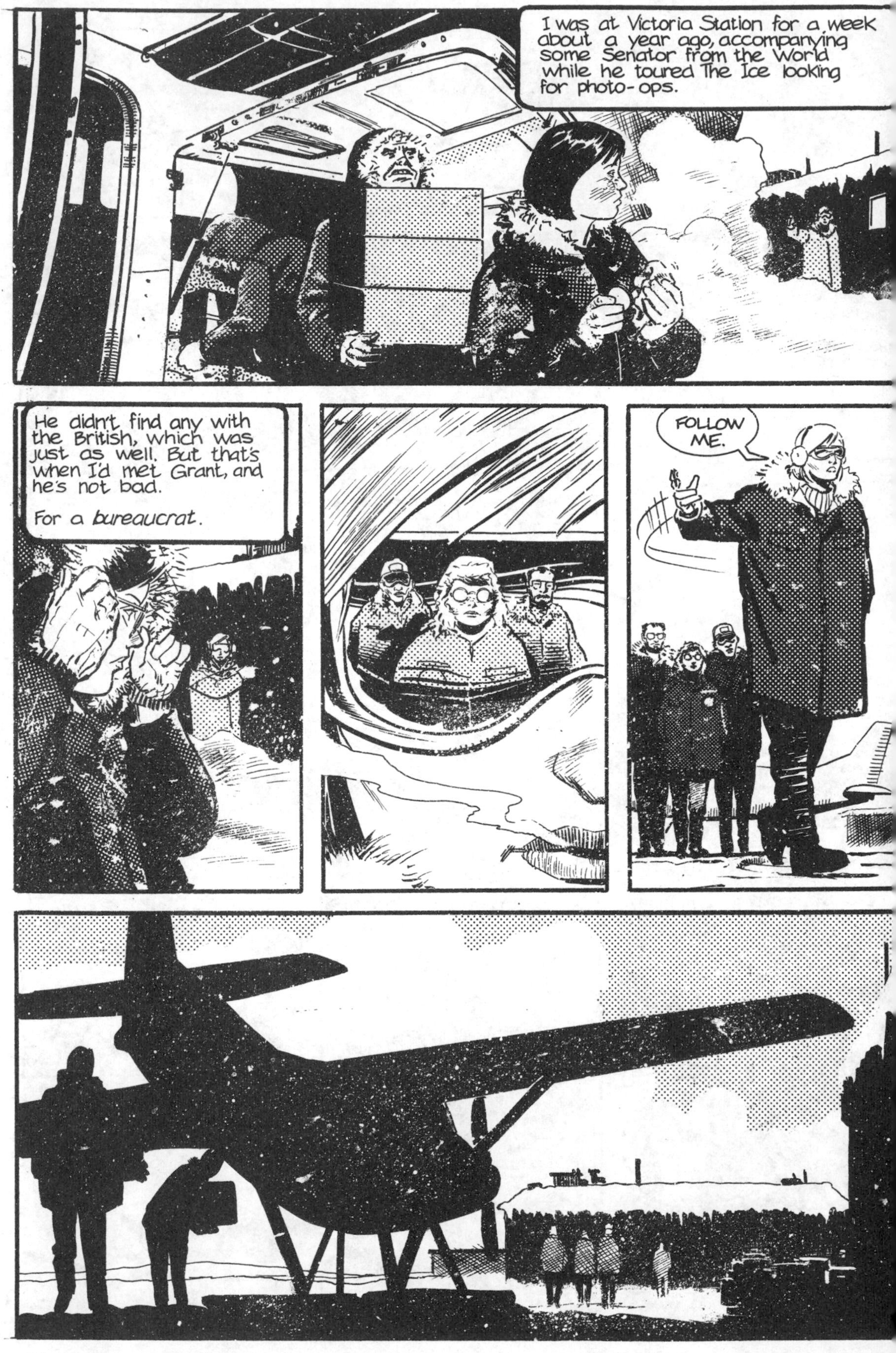
I was at Victoria Station for a week about a year ago, accompanying some Senator from the World while he toured The Ice looking for photo-ops.
He didn't find any with the British, which was just as well. But that's when I'd met Grant, and he's not bad.
For a *bureaucrat*.
FOLLOW ME.

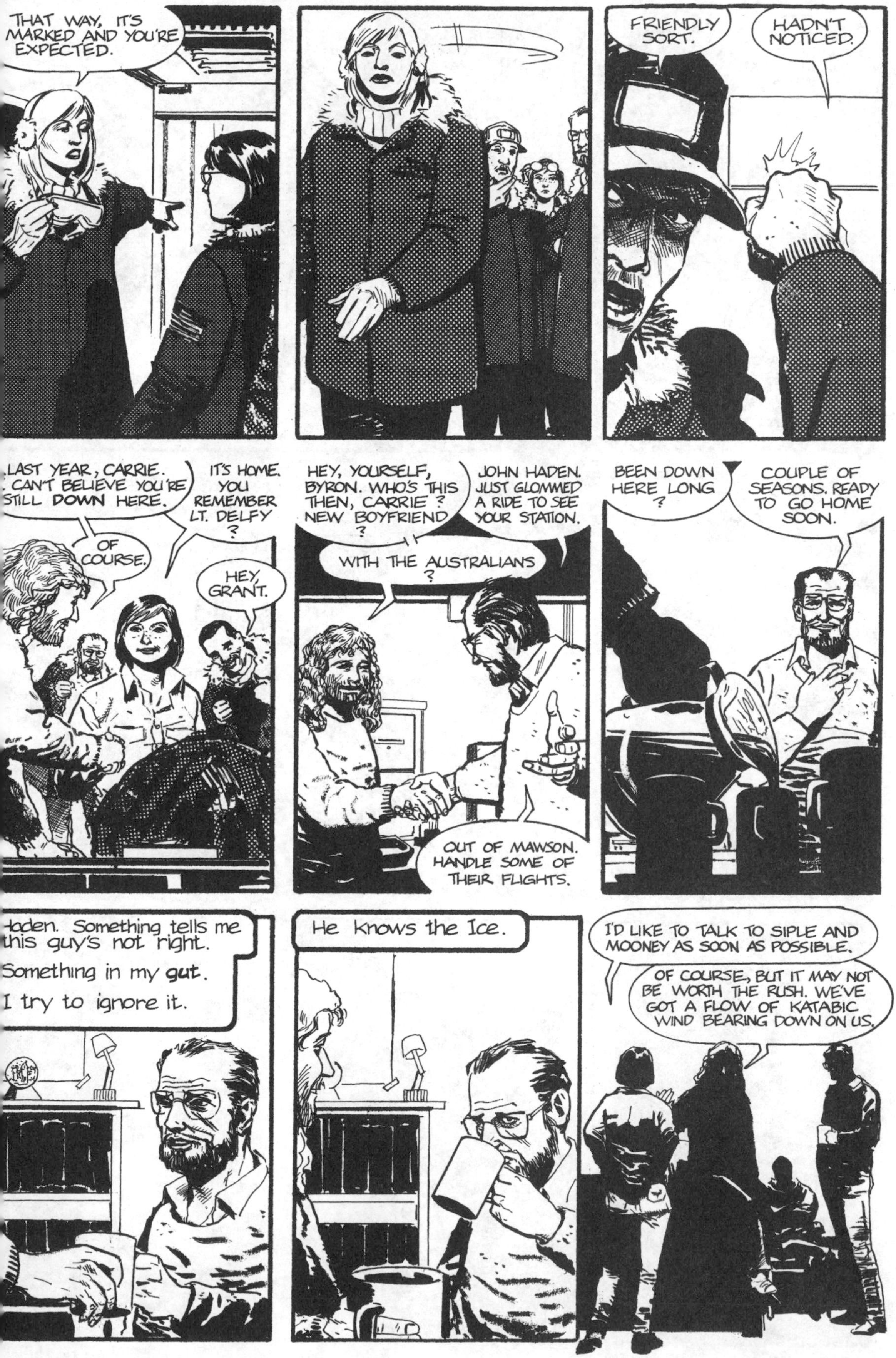
THAT WAY, IT'S MARKED AND YOU'RE EXPECTED.
FRIENDLY SORT.
HADN'T NOTICED.
LAST YEAR, CARRIE. CAN'T BELIEVE YOU'RE STILL DOWN HERE.
IT'S HOME. YOU REMEMBER LT. DELFY?
OF COURSE.
HEY, GRANT.
HEY, YOURSELF, BYRON. WHO'S THIS THEN, CARRIE? NEW BOYFRIEND?
JOHN HADEN. JUST GLOMMED A RIDE TO SEE YOUR STATION.
WITH THE AUSTRALIANS?
OUT OF MAWSON. HANDLE SOME OF THEIR FLIGHTS.
BEEN DOWN HERE LONG?
COUPLE OF SEASONS. READY TO GO HOME SOON.
Haden. Something tells me this guy's not right.
Something in my gut.
I try to ignore it.
He knows the Ice.
I'D LIKE TO TALK TO SIPLE AND MOONEY AS SOON AS POSSIBLE.
OF COURSE, BUT IT MAY NOT BE WORTH THE RUSH. WE'VE GOT A FLOW OF KATABIC WIND BEARING DOWN ON US.

"...LOOKS LIKE WE'LL BE IN A WHITEOUT. NO IDEA HOW LONG IT COULD LAST.

I **TRIED** TO TELL HER WE WERE GOING TO BE STUCK HERE. SHE DIDN'T **LISTEN.**

YOU'RE **POSITIVE** YOU DON'T WANT TO WAIT? **WITH** THE STORM COMING, **CERTAINLY** NOT GOING ANYWHERE.

YOU DON'T WITH THE THEY'RE GOING

THE **SOONER** I CAN TALK TO THEM, THE **BETTER.**

WHAT'S THE **RUSH?**

BUSINESS.

**GRANT?** CAN WE GET **ON** WITH IT?

YOU GO OUT THERE, IT WON'T BE OUR RESPONSIBILITY **WHATEVER** HAPPENS TO YOU.

I **KNOW** THE DRILL.

**SHARPE** WILL TAKE YOU TO SEE THEM. SHOULD BE IN THE **LOUNGE.**

He's covering his ass.

I shouldn't hold it against him.

But I do.

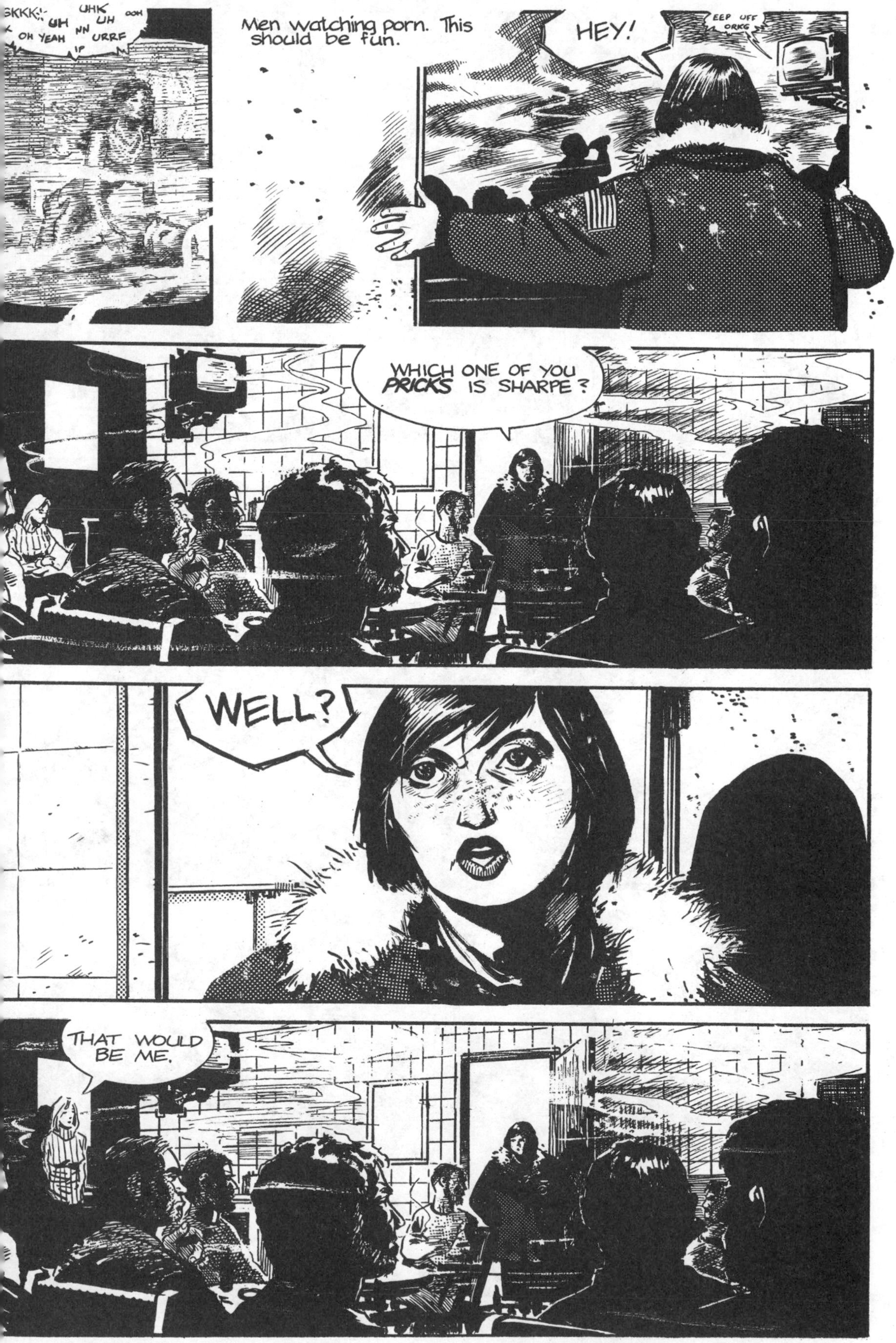
SKKK!-
UH
UHK
UH
OOH
OH YEAH
NN
URRF
IP
Men watching porn. This should be fun.
HEY!
EEP UFF ORKG
WHICH ONE OF YOU PRICKS IS SHARPE?
WELL?
THAT WOULD BE ME.

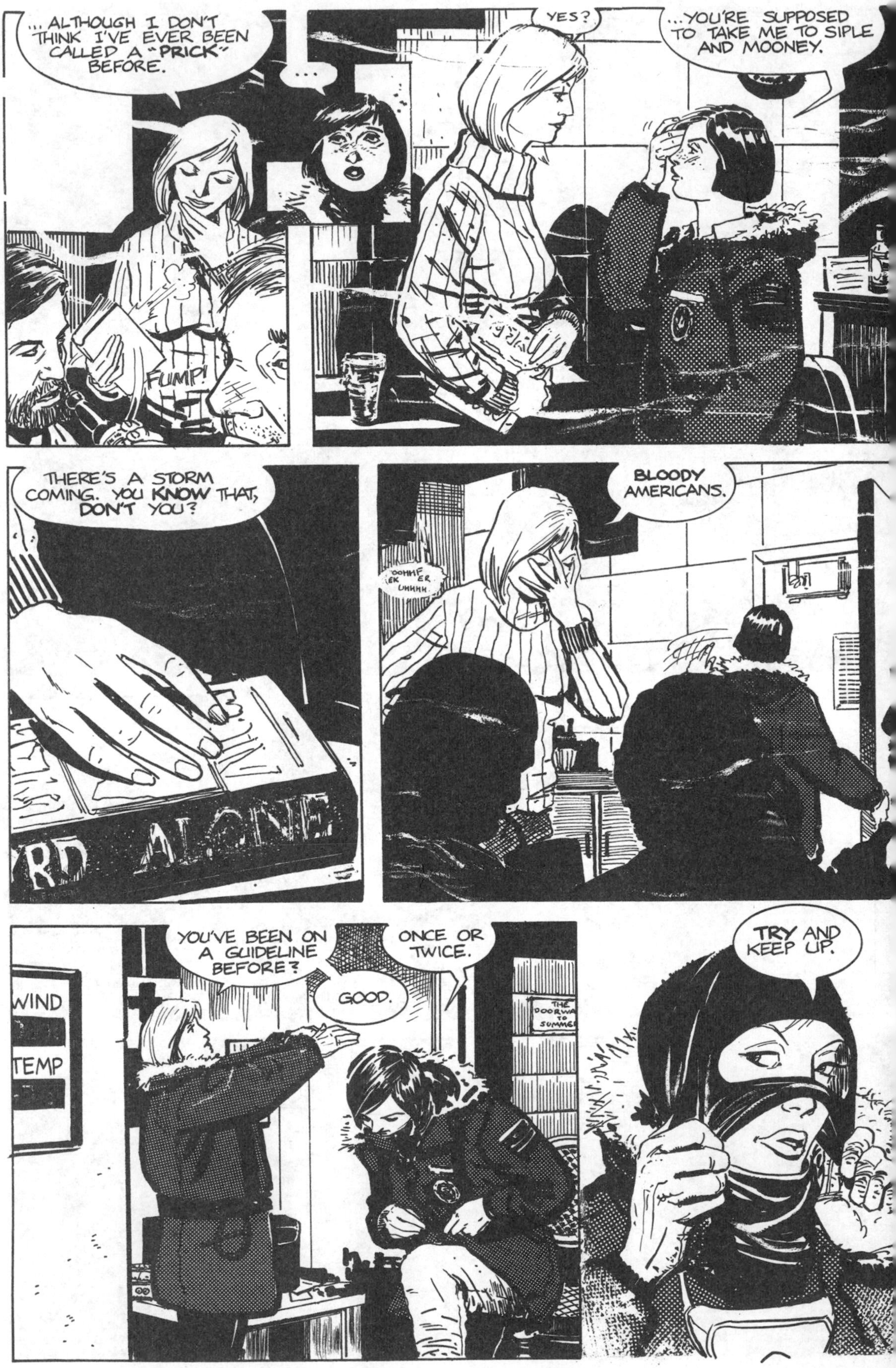
...ALTHOUGH I DON'T THINK I'VE EVER BEEN CALLED A "PRICK" BEFORE.
...
FUMP!
YES?
...YOU'RE SUPPOSED TO TAKE ME TO SIPLE AND MOONEY.
THERE'S A STORM COMING. YOU KNOW THAT, DON'T YOU?
RD ALONE
BLOODY AMERICANS.
WIND
TEMP
YOU'VE BEEN ON A GUIDELINE BEFORE?
ONCE OR TWICE.
GOOD.
TRY AND KEEP UP.

Wind chill...

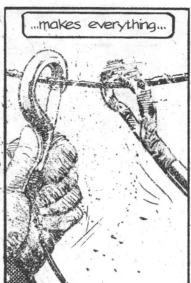

...makes everything...

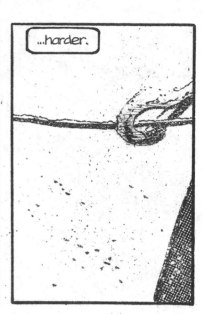

...harder.

The **third** time the wind almost lifts me off the ground, I start reconsidering...

Why am I doing this?

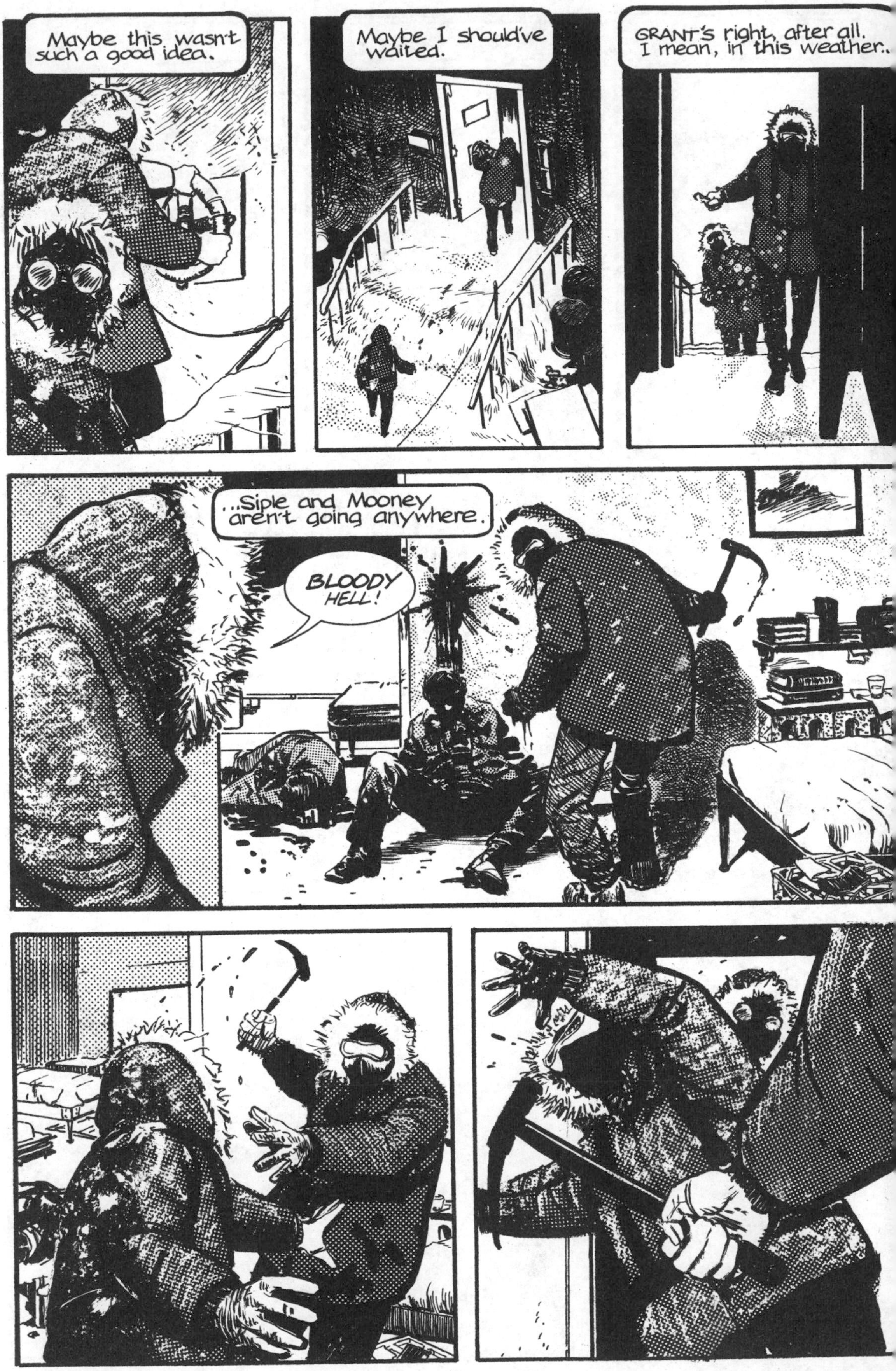

Maybe this wasn't such a good idea.
Maybe I should've waited.
GRANT's right, after all. I mean, in this weather..
...Siple and Mooney aren't going anywhere.
BLOODY HELL!

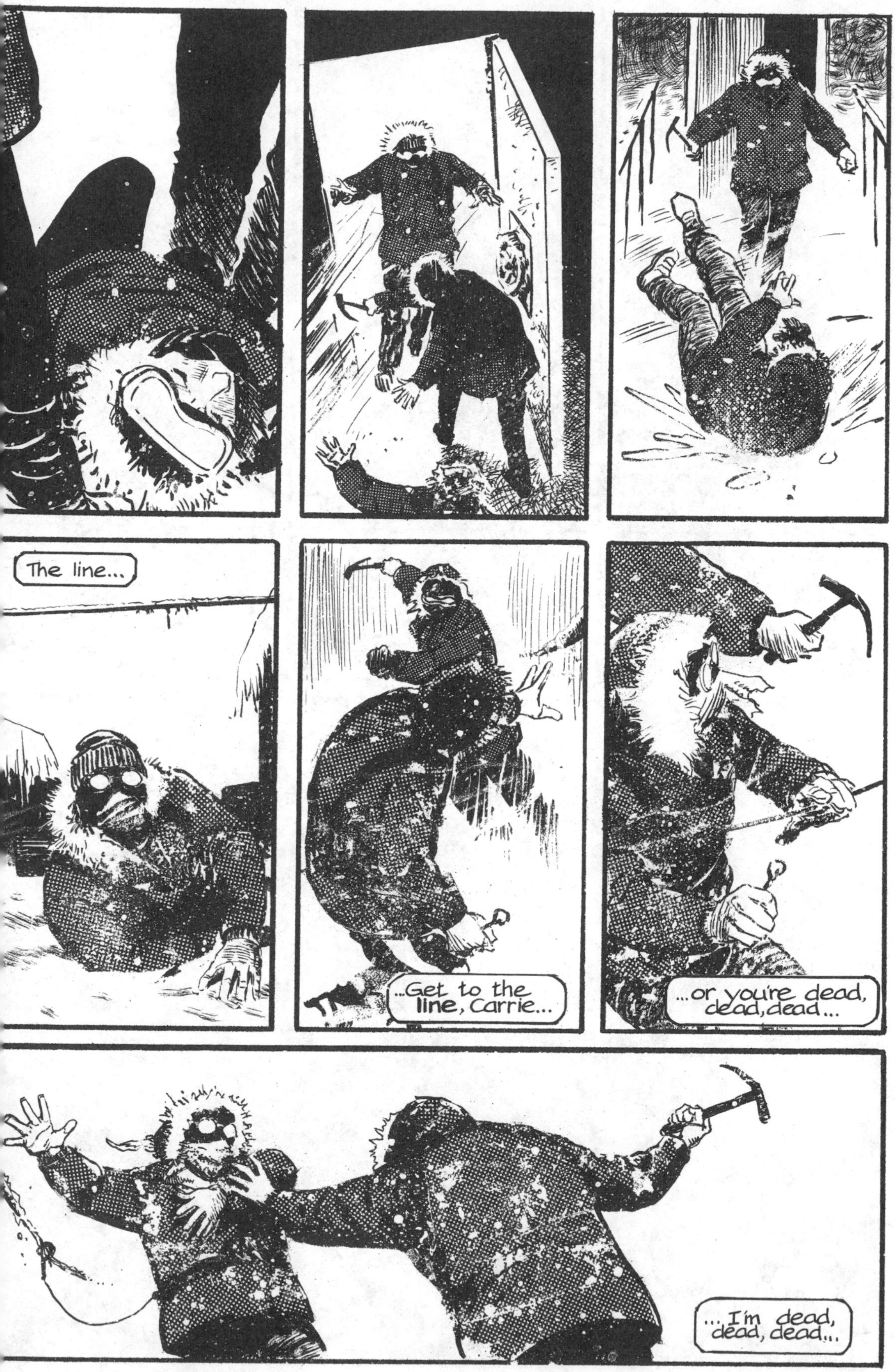
The line...
...Get to the line, Carrie...
...or you're dead, dead, dead...
...I'm dead, dead, dead...

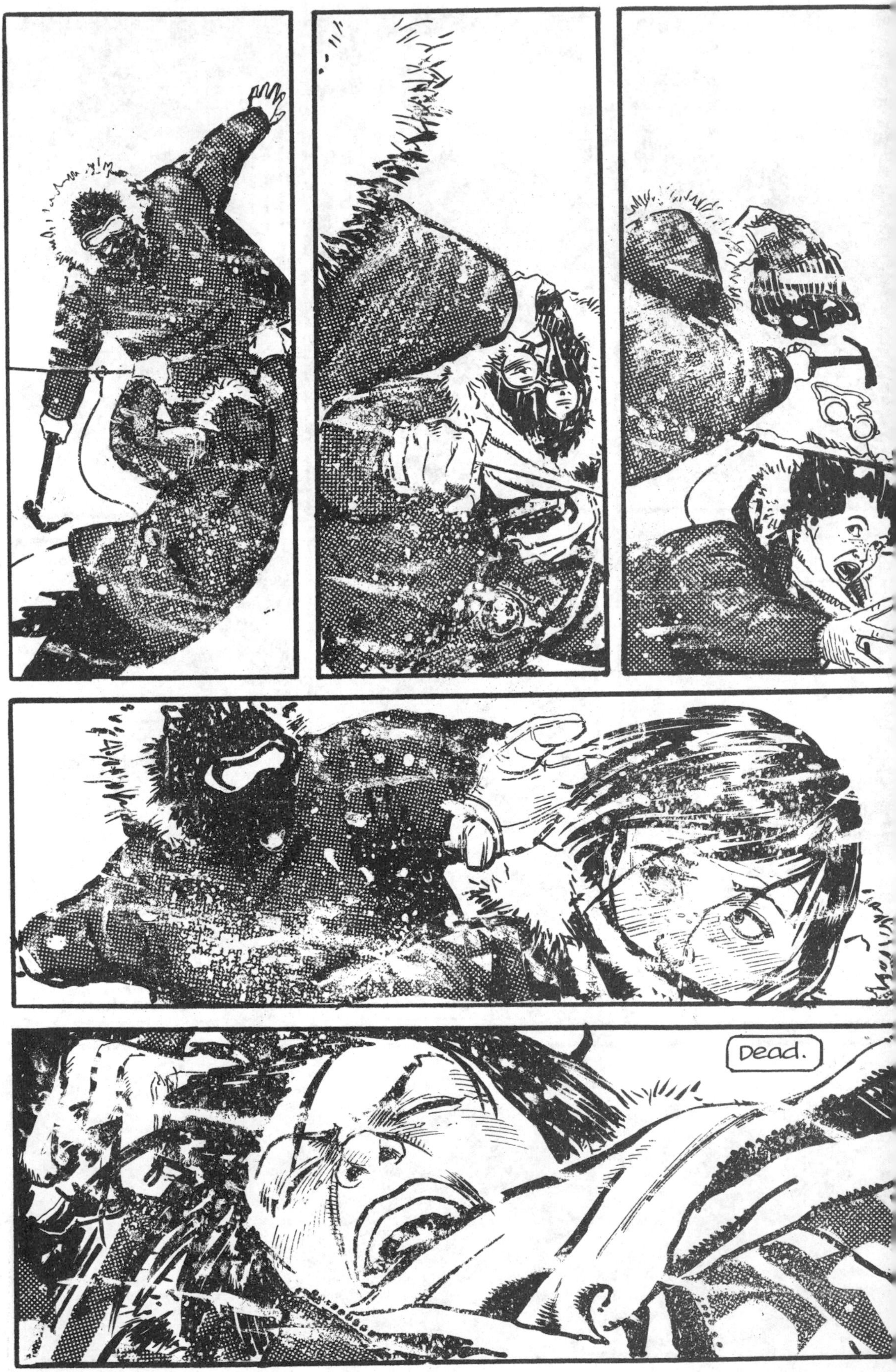
Dead.

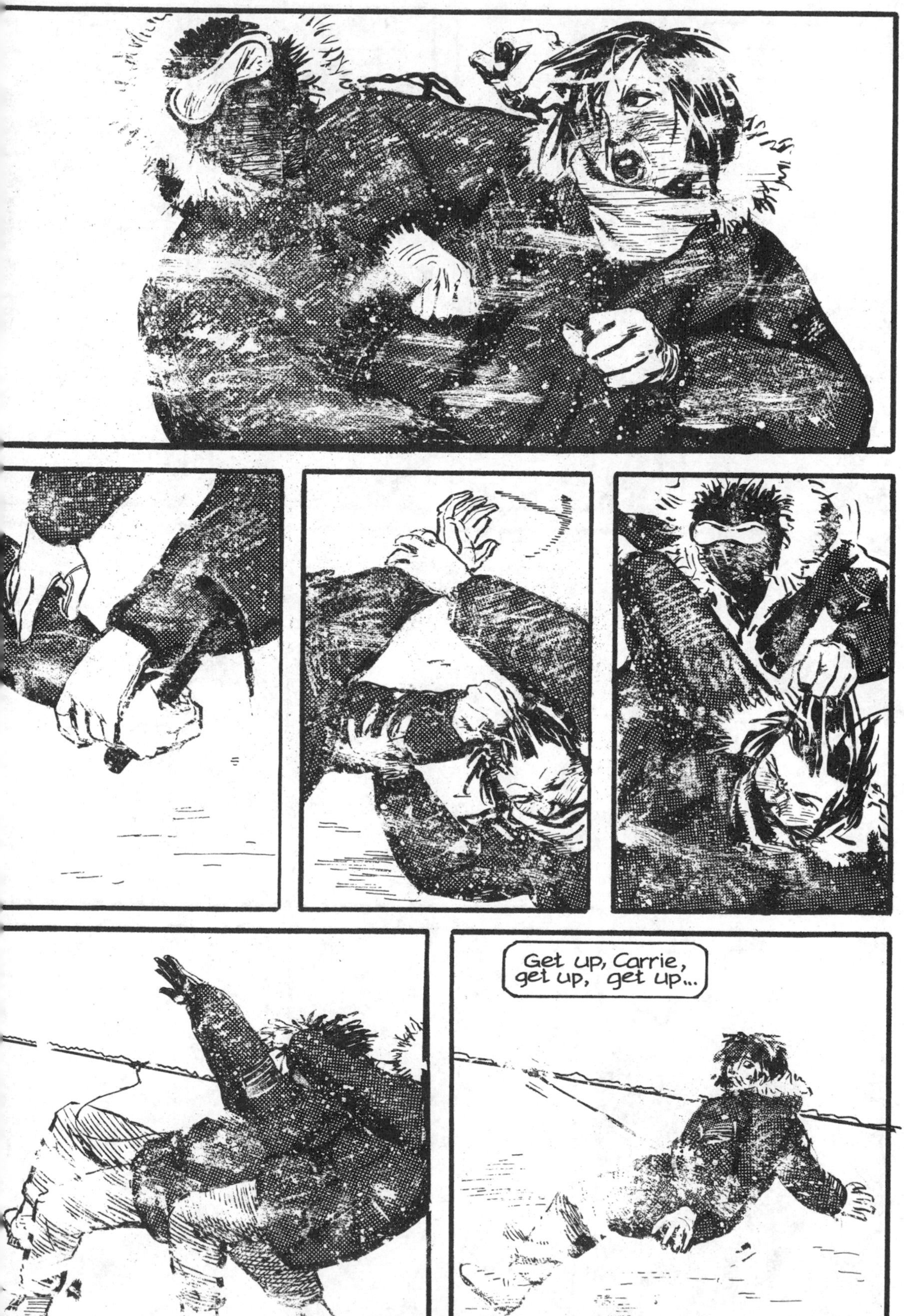
Get up, Carrie,
get up, get up...

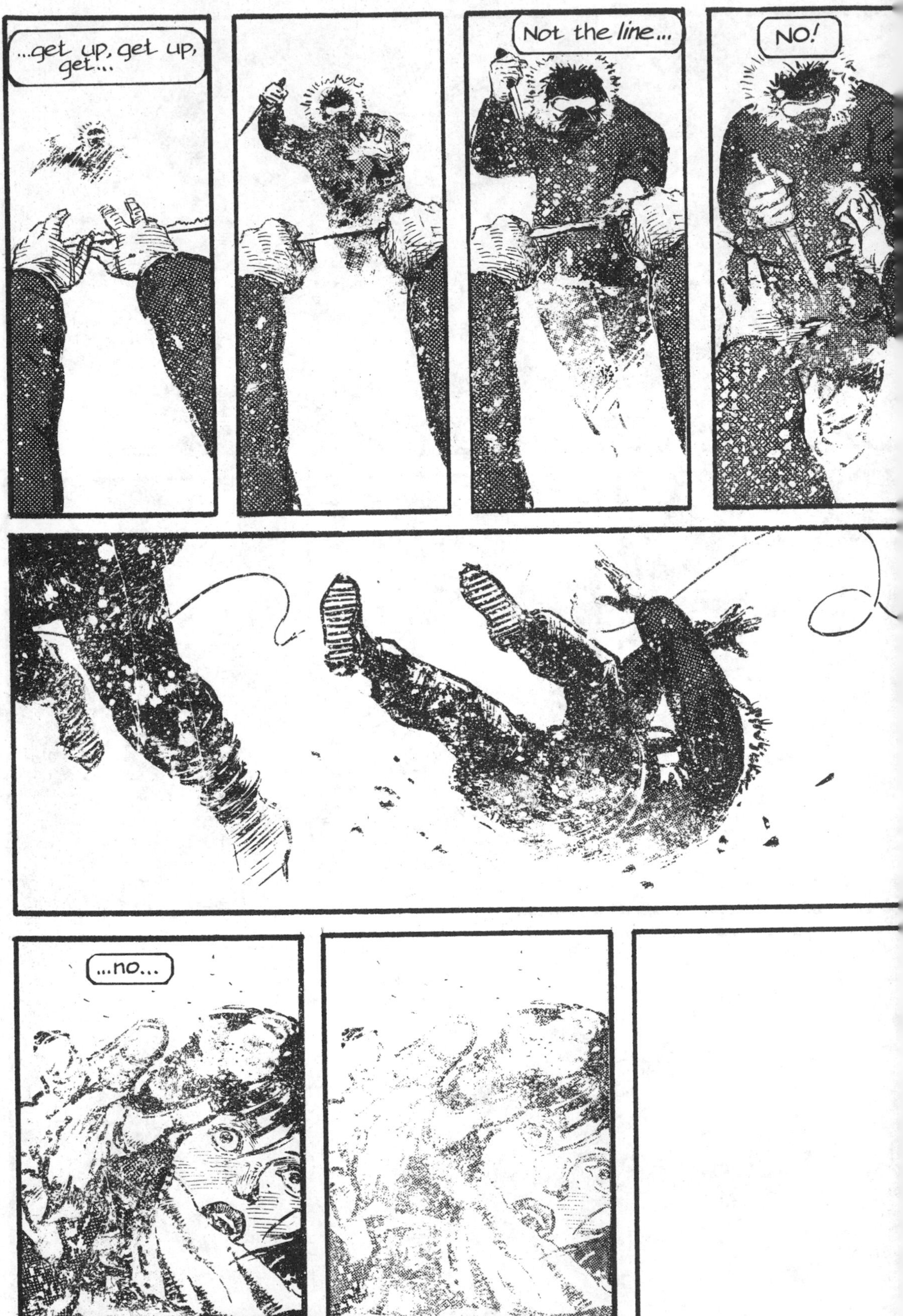
...get up, get up, get...
Not the *line*...
NO!
...no...

*End of part one.*

# CHAPTER TWO

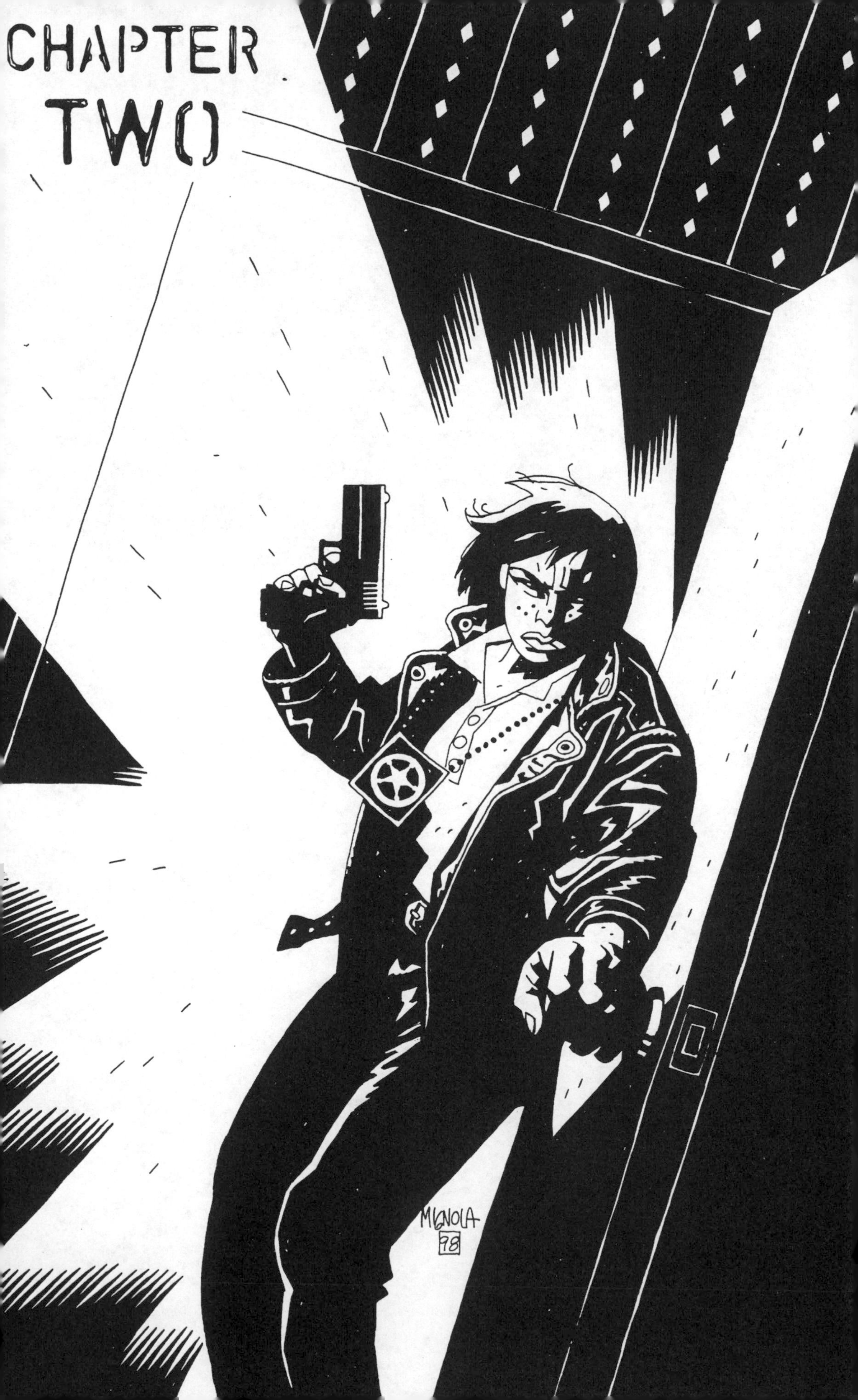
MIGNOLA
98

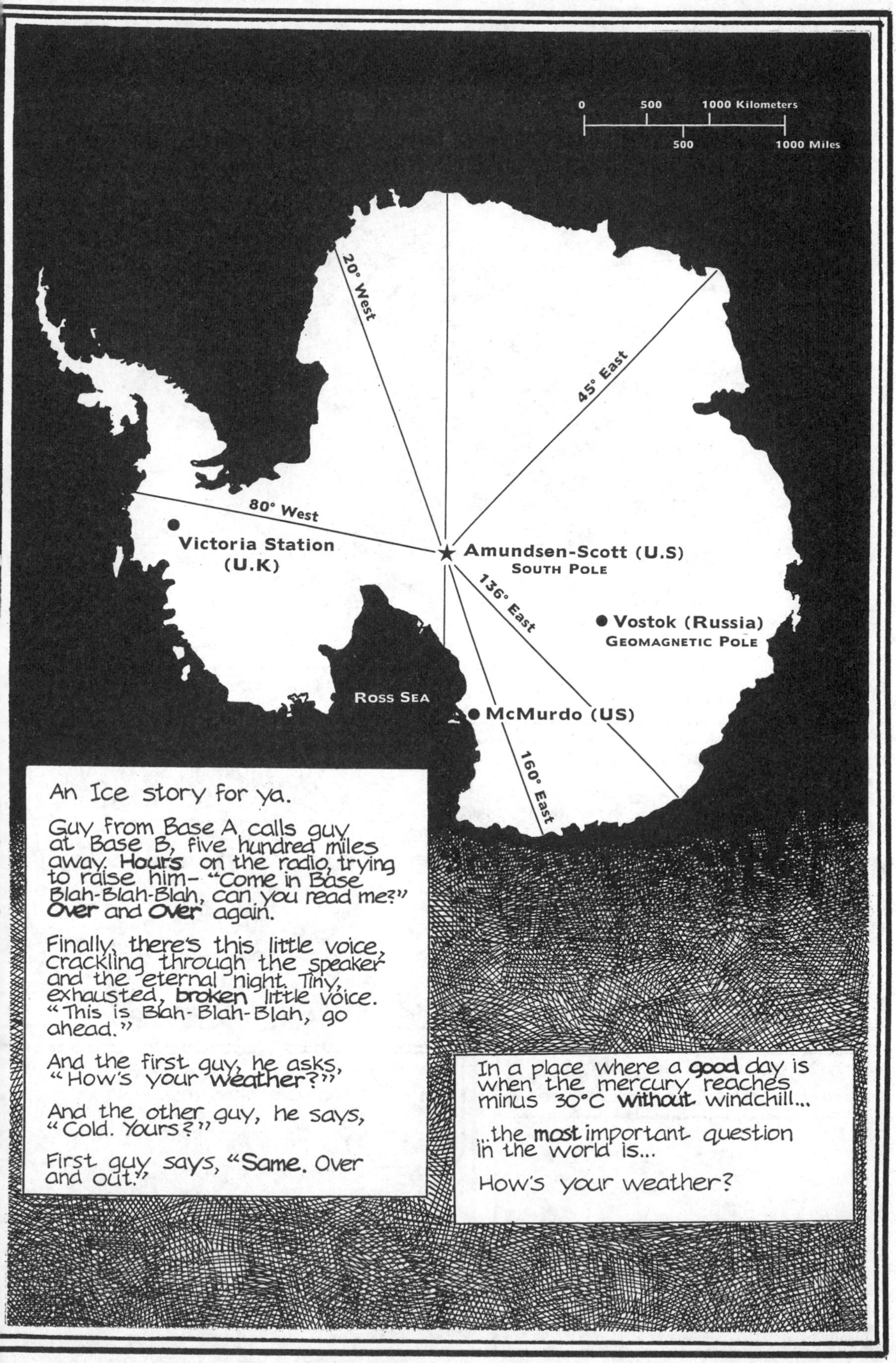
0
500
1000 Kilometers
500
1000 Miles
20° West
45° East
80° West
Victoria Station (U.K)
Amundsen-Scott (U.S)
South Pole
136° East
Vostok (Russia)
Geomagnetic Pole
Ross Sea
McMurdo (US)
160° East
An Ice story for ya.
Guy from Base A calls guy at Base B, five hundred miles away. **Hours** on the radio, trying to raise him– "Come in Base Blah-Blah-Blah, can you read me?" **Over** and **Over** again.
Finally, there's this little voice, crackling through the speaker and the eternal night. Tiny, exhausted, **broken** little voice. "This is Blah-Blah-Blah, go ahead."
And the first guy, he asks, "How's your **weather**?"
And the other guy, he says, "Cold. Yours?"
First guy says, "**Same.** Over and out."
In a place where a **good** day is when the mercury reaches minus 30°C **without** windchill...
...the **most** important question in the world is...
How's your weather?

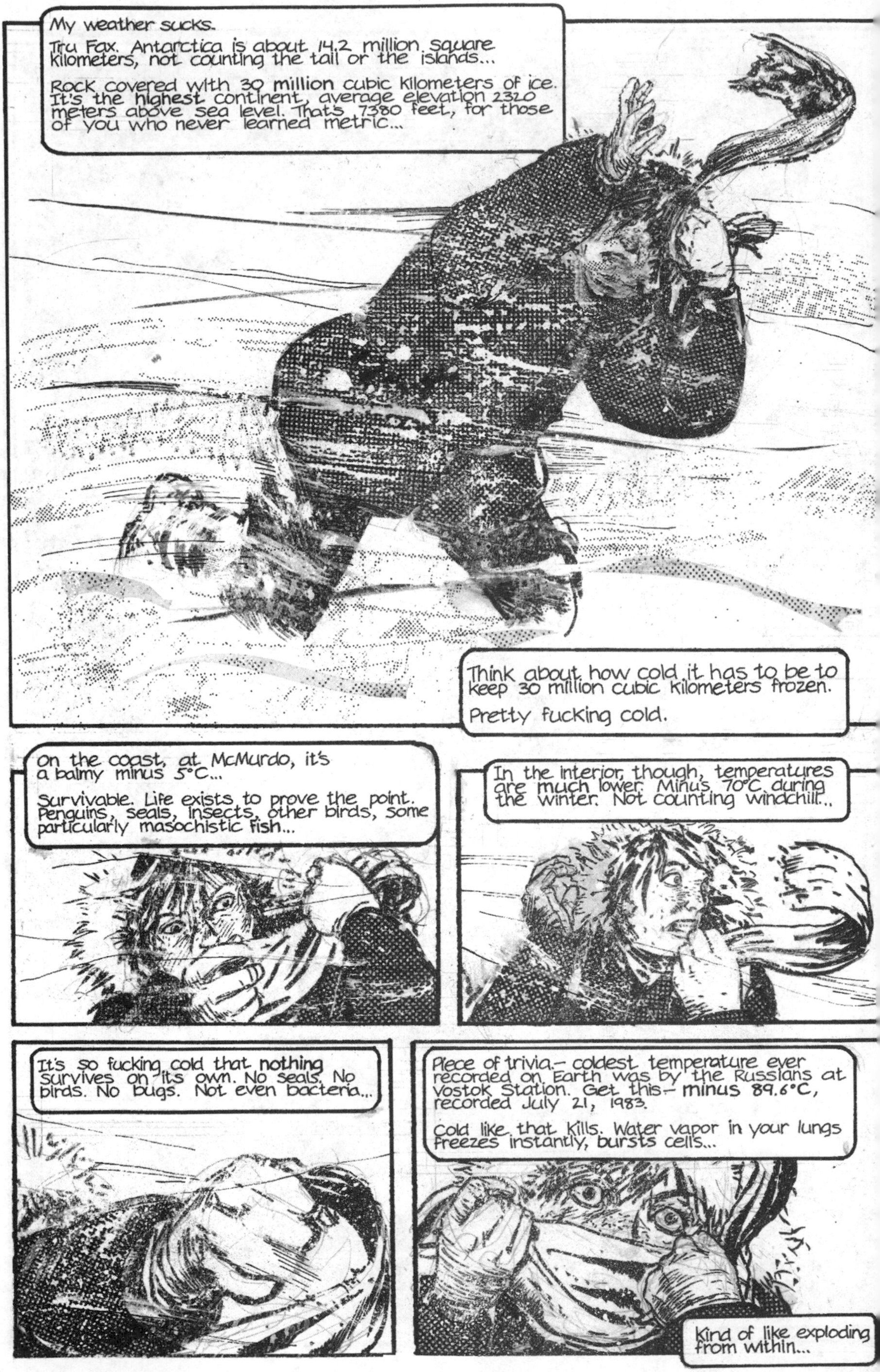
My weather sucks.
Tru Fax. Antarctica is about 14.2 million square kilometers, not counting the tail or the islands...
Rock covered with 30 million cubic kilometers of ice. It's the highest continent, average elevation 2320 meters above sea level. That's 7380 feet, for those of you who never learned metric...
Think about how cold it has to be to keep 30 million cubic kilometers frozen.
Pretty fucking cold.
On the coast, at McMurdo, it's a balmy minus 5°C...
Survivable. Life exists to prove the point. Penguins, seals, insects, other birds, some particularly masochistic fish...
In the interior, though, temperatures are much lower. Minus 70°C during the winter. Not counting windchill...
It's so fucking cold that nothing survives on its own. No seals. No birds. No bugs. Not even bacteria...
Piece of trivia— coldest temperature ever recorded on Earth was by the Russians at Vostok Station. Get this— minus 89.6°C, recorded July 21, 1983.
Cold like that kills. Water vapor in your lungs freezes instantly, bursts cells...
Kind of like exploding from within...

Vostok's in the **interior**, in case you couldn't guess.

And that record, that's **not** counting windchill. And it gets windy...

Sorry, did I say windy?

The Ice is the windiest place on earth. **Katabic winds**, blowing from the Polar plateau down to the ocean. Fast.

320 kilometers an hour fast, sometimes.

With that sort of windchill, the temp plummets into the triple-digits.

Wind kicks up snow that's lain on the Ice for thousands of years, **tosses** it through the air. Destroys visibility, you can't see six inches in front of you, can't tell the ground from the sky.

That's called a **whiteout**.

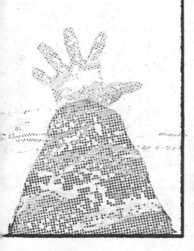

People freeze to death in whiteouts...

...bodies found a **foot** from safety and warmth...

...died because they couldn't see the damn front door...

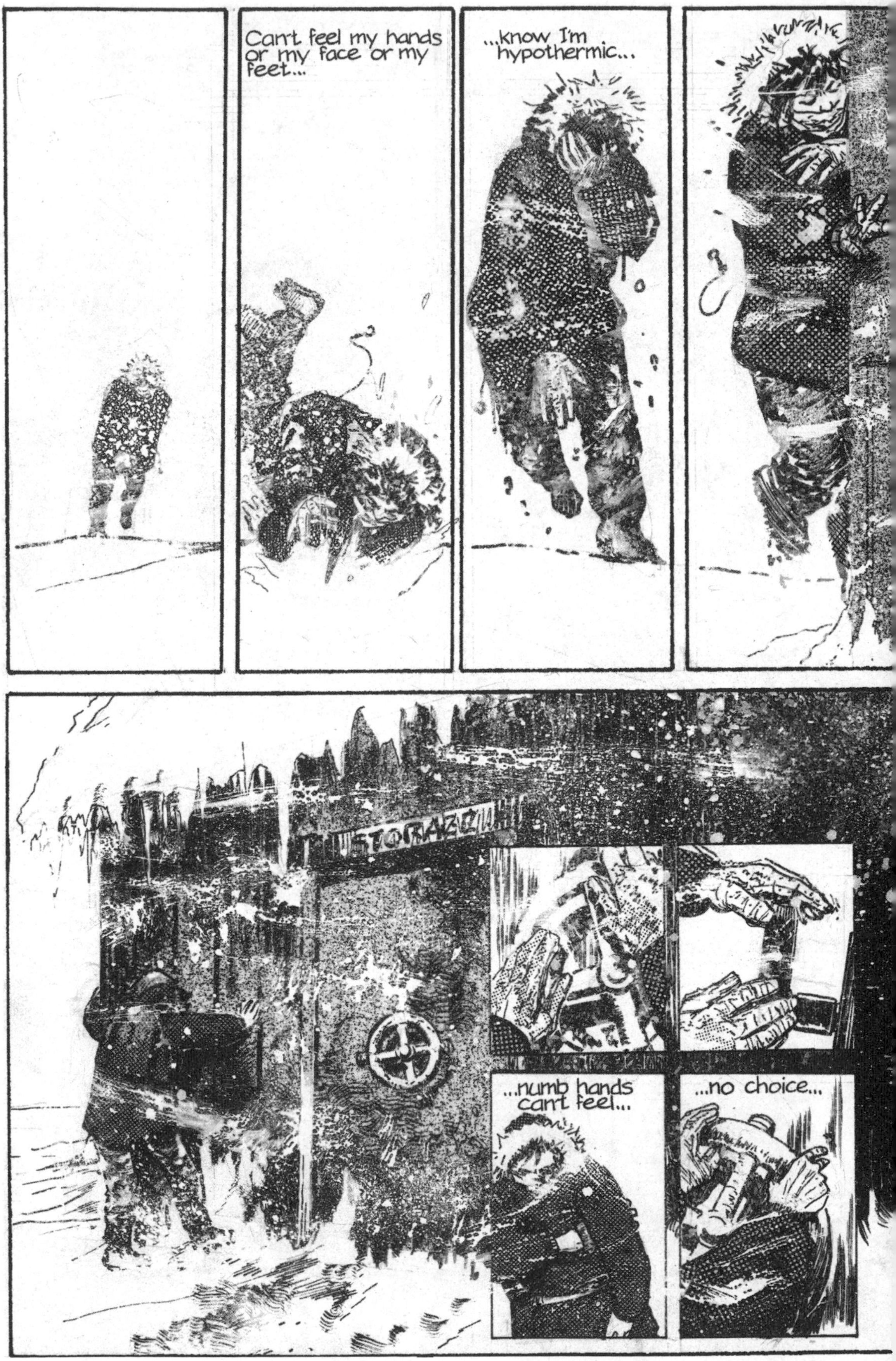
Can't feel my hands or my face or my feet...
...know I'm hypothermic...
STORAGE
...numb hands can't feel...
...no choice...

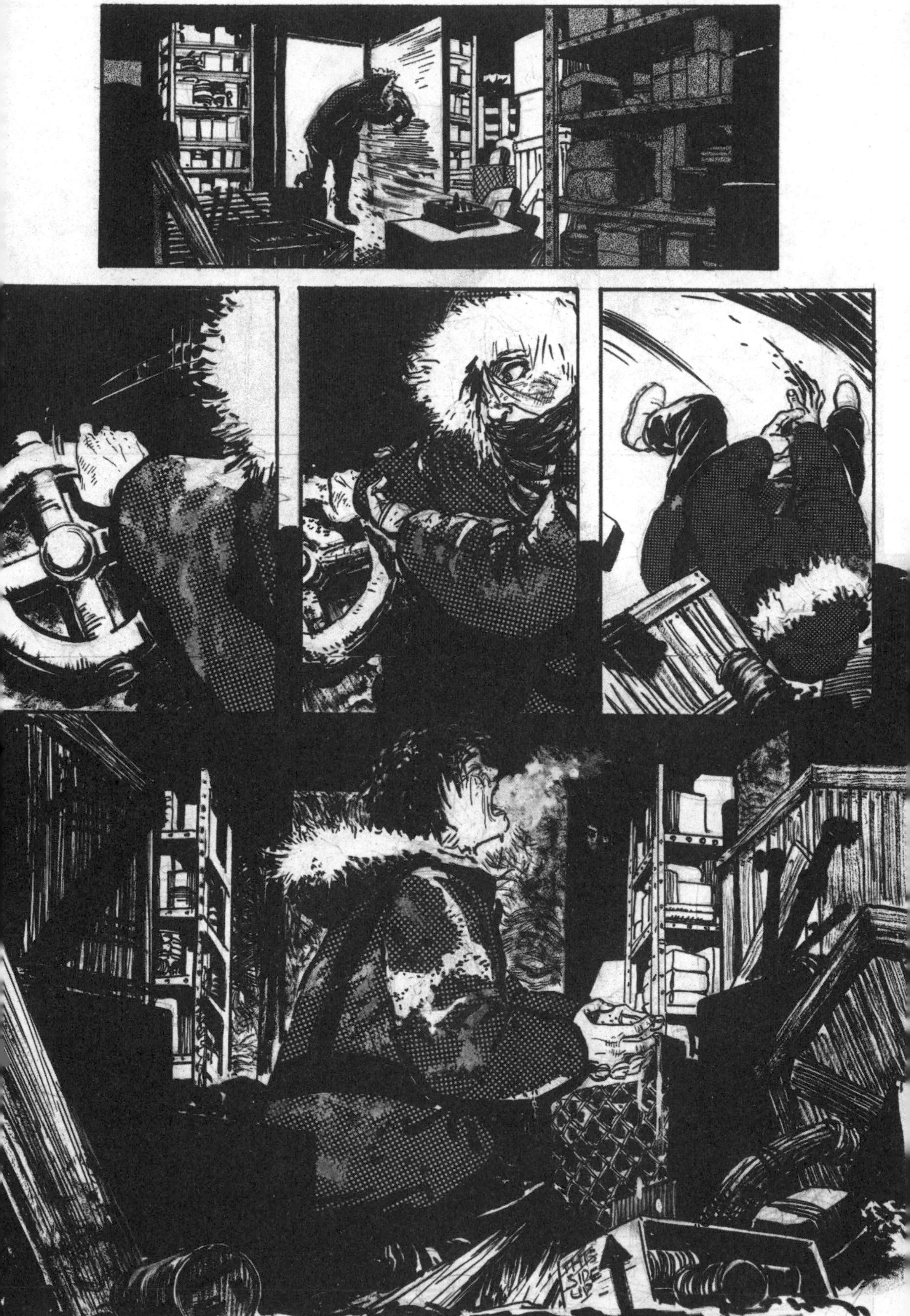
THIS SIDE UP

I've been knocked out *three* times before. Twice in training...

...and then once again last year in Macao.

Every time I come to, I do the same bloody thing...

...I puke.

It also takes a minute for the synapses to come back on-line, for the short-term memory to return.

MARSHAL?

This is not good...

If the Marshal's not in here, then she's out there...

...she had the guideline, she should be fine.

Interesting. McMurdo again. Why?

SIPLE
MOONEY
RUBIN
KELLER ← McM
WEISS
WESSELHOFT.

Swings shut on its own, to preserve the integrity of the heat-lock...

...or not.

Oh, most definitely not good.

Wind's dying. Or maybe I'm going deaf.

It could be hours, maybe days, before anyone can make it outside to look for me.

Hypothermia is insidious.

It makes you see things.

It makes you not care.

I stopped shivering an hour ago.

I'm not cold anymore.

EMERGENCY SUPPLIES

HOT LITTLE NUMBER, AREN'T YOU?

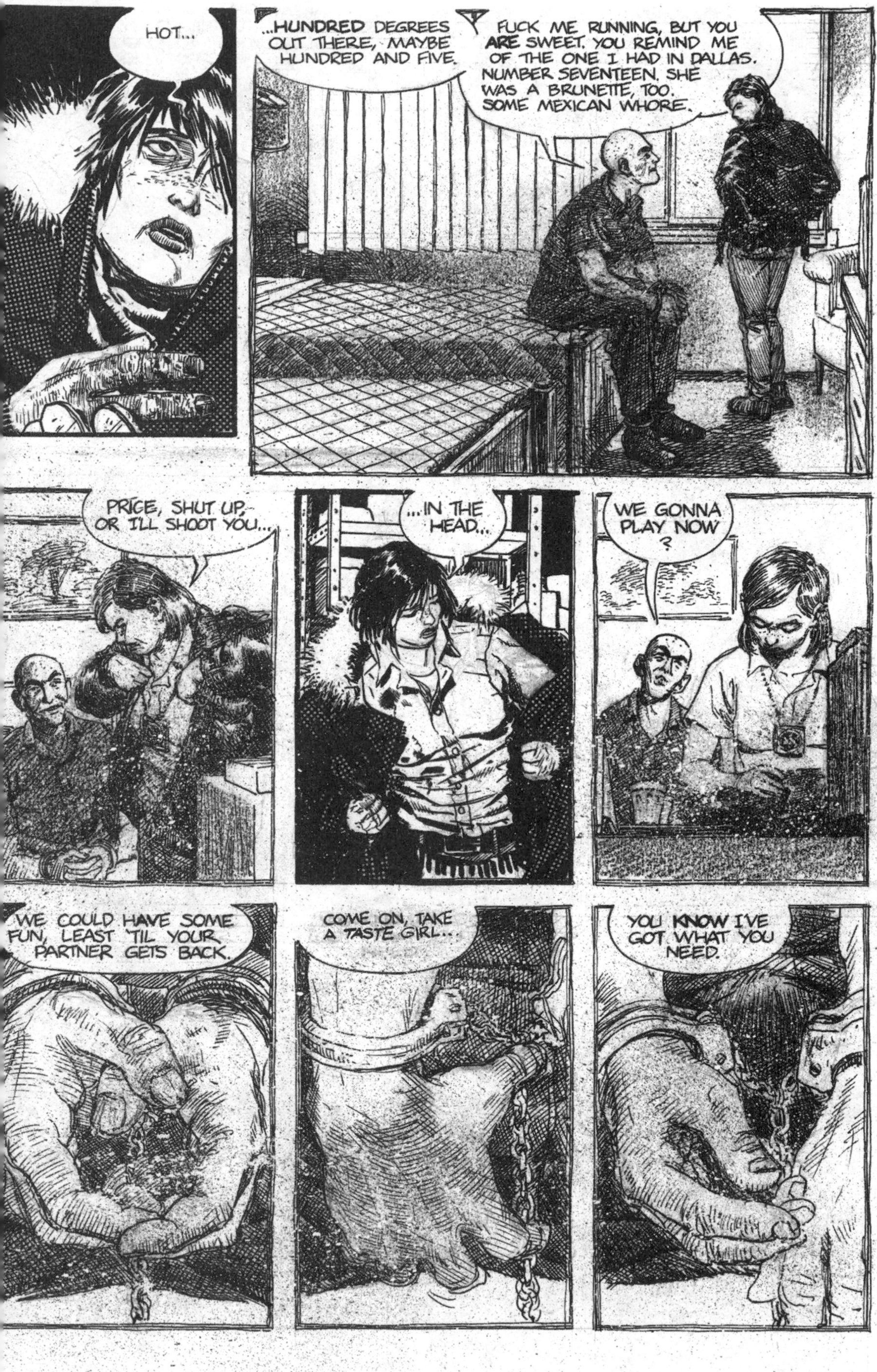
HOT...
...HUNDRED DEGREES OUT THERE, MAYBE HUNDRED AND FIVE.
FUCK ME RUNNING, BUT YOU ARE SWEET. YOU REMIND ME OF THE ONE I HAD IN DALLAS. NUMBER SEVENTEEN. SHE WAS A BRUNETTE, TOO. SOME MEXICAN WHORE.
PRICE, SHUT UP, OR I'LL SHOOT YOU...
...IN THE HEAD...
WE GONNA PLAY NOW ?
WE COULD HAVE SOME FUN, LEAST 'TIL YOUR PARTNER GETS BACK.
COME ON, TAKE A TASTE GIRL...
YOU KNOW I'VE GOT WHAT YOU NEED.

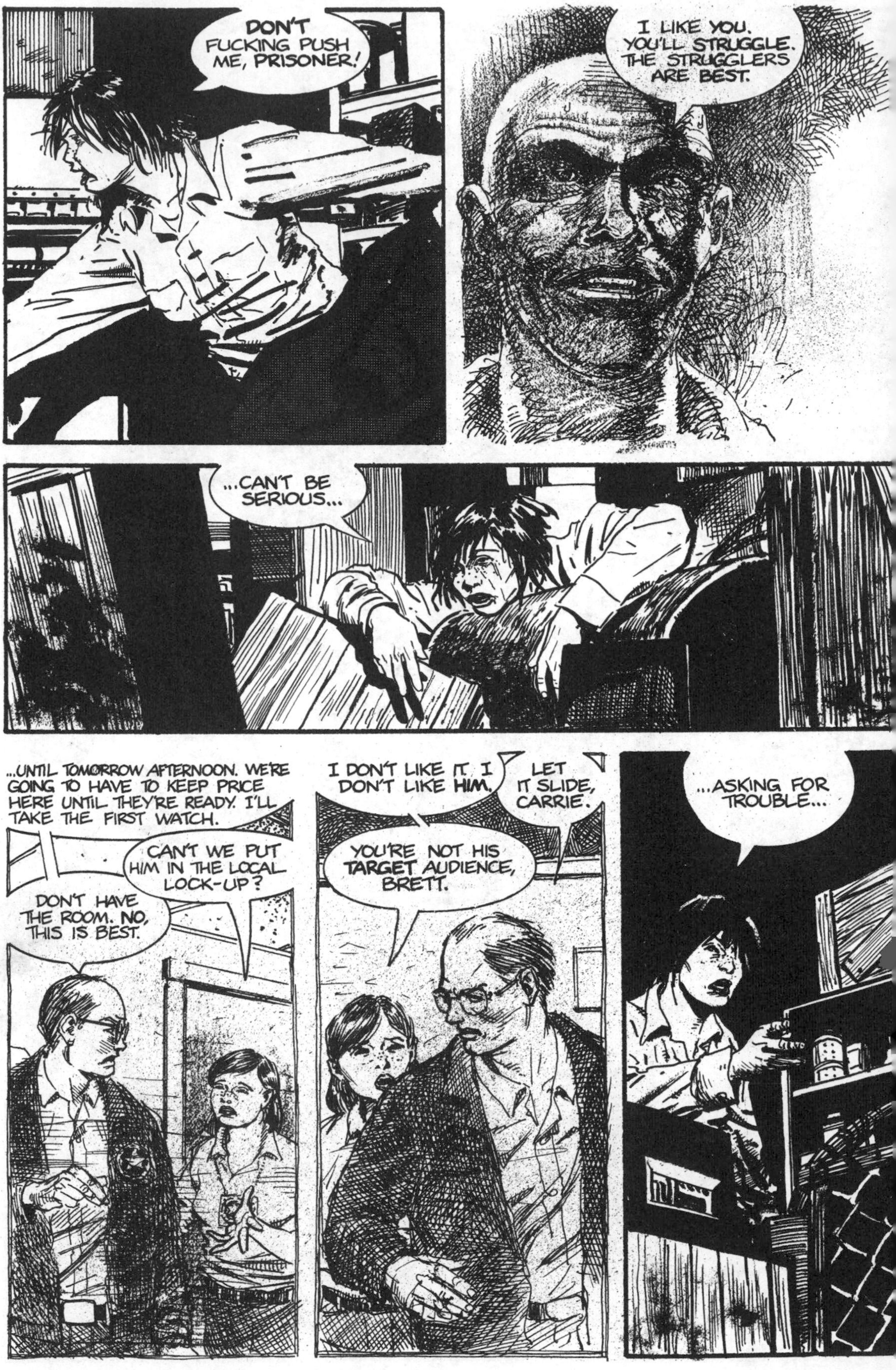
DON'T FUCKING PUSH ME, PRISONER!
I LIKE YOU. YOU'LL STRUGGLE. THE STRUGGLERS ARE BEST.
...CAN'T BE SERIOUS...
...UNTIL TOMORROW AFTERNOON. WE'RE GOING TO HAVE TO KEEP PRICE HERE UNTIL THEY'RE READY. I'LL TAKE THE FIRST WATCH.
CAN'T WE PUT HIM IN THE LOCAL LOCK-UP?
DON'T HAVE THE ROOM. NO, THIS IS BEST.
I DON'T LIKE IT. I DON'T LIKE HIM.
YOU'RE NOT HIS TARGET AUDIENCE, BRETT.
LET IT SLIDE, CARRIE.
...ASKING FOR TROUBLE...

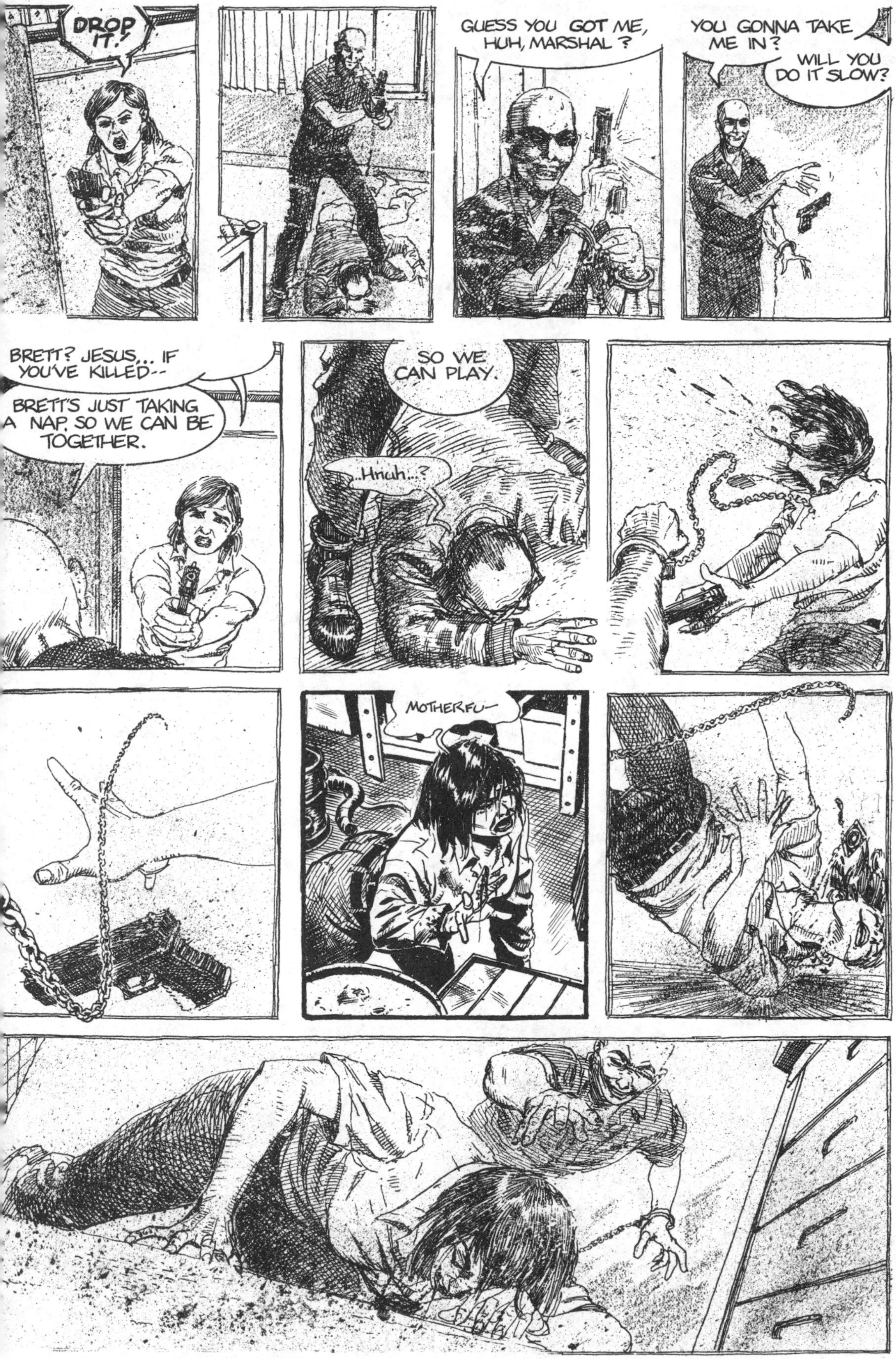
DROP IT.
GUESS YOU GOT ME, HUH, MARSHAL ?
YOU GONNA TAKE ME IN?
WILL YOU DO IT SLOW?
BRETT? JESUS... IF YOU'VE KILLED--
BRETT'S JUST TAKING A NAP. SO WE CAN BE TOGETHER.
SO WE CAN PLAY.
...Hnuh...?
MOTHERFU--

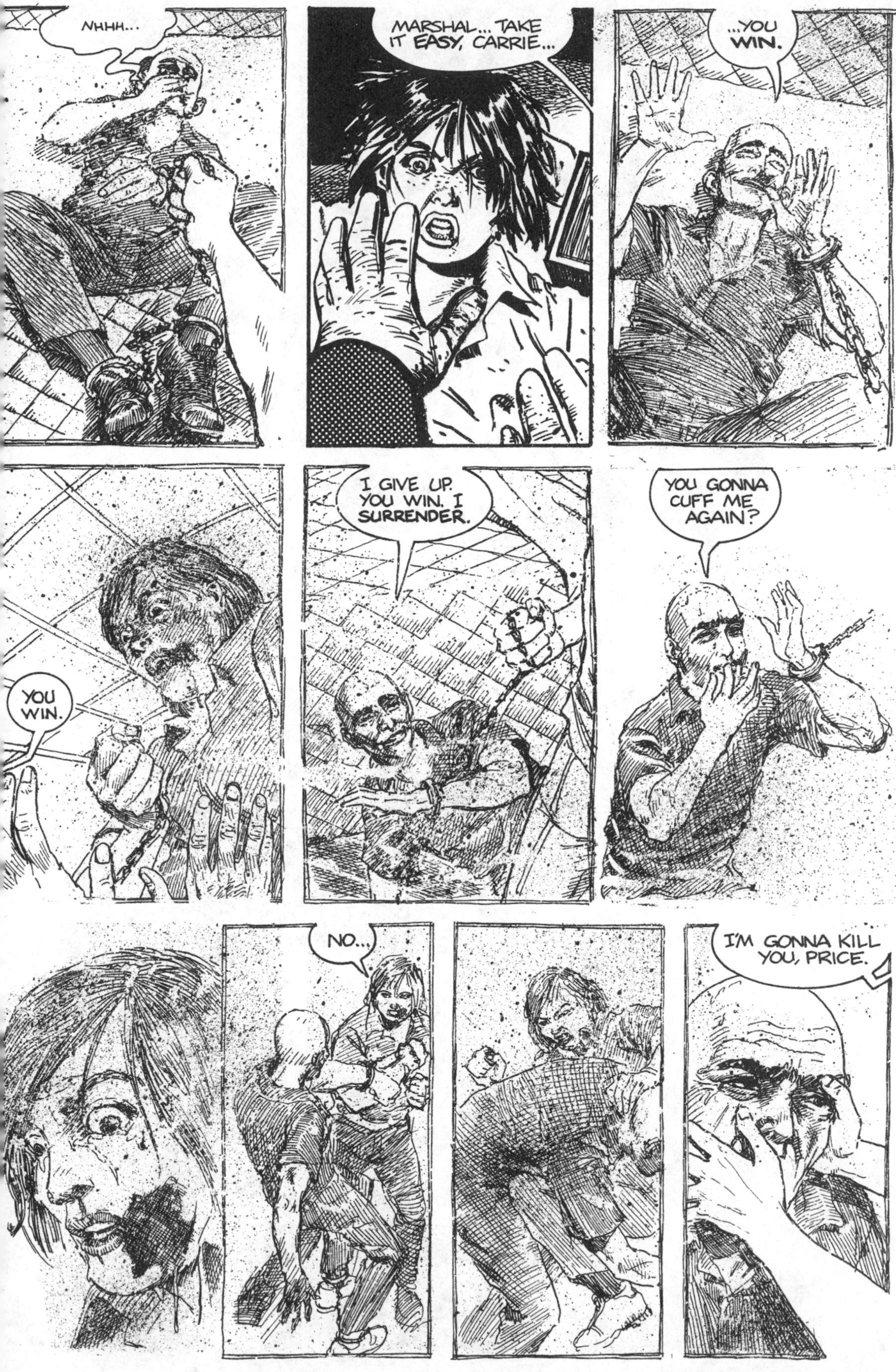
NHHH...
MARSHAL... TAKE IT EASY, CARRIE...
...YOU WIN.
YOU WIN.
I GIVE UP. YOU WIN. I SURRENDER.
YOU GONNA CUFF ME AGAIN?
NO...
I'M GONNA KILL YOU, PRICE.

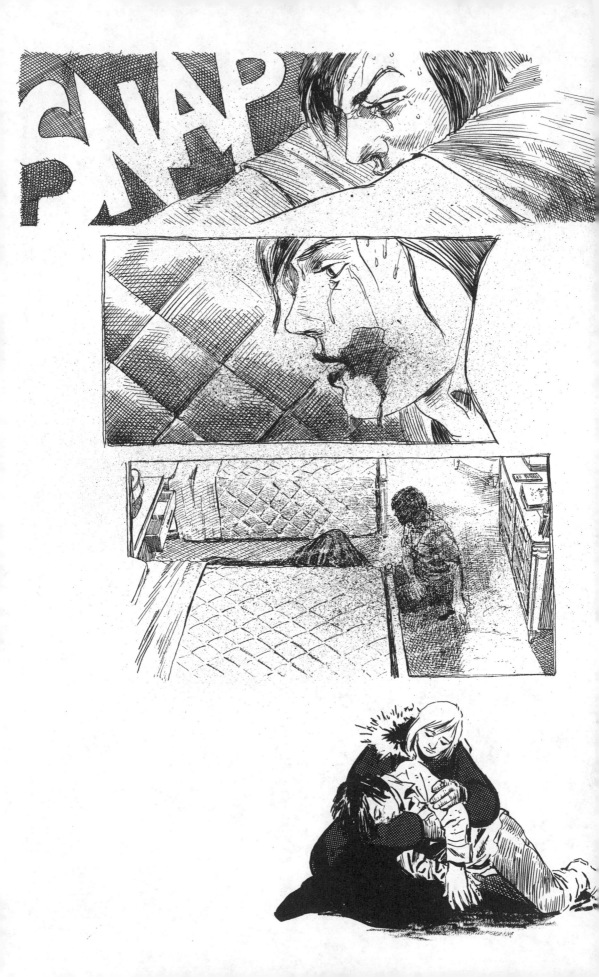

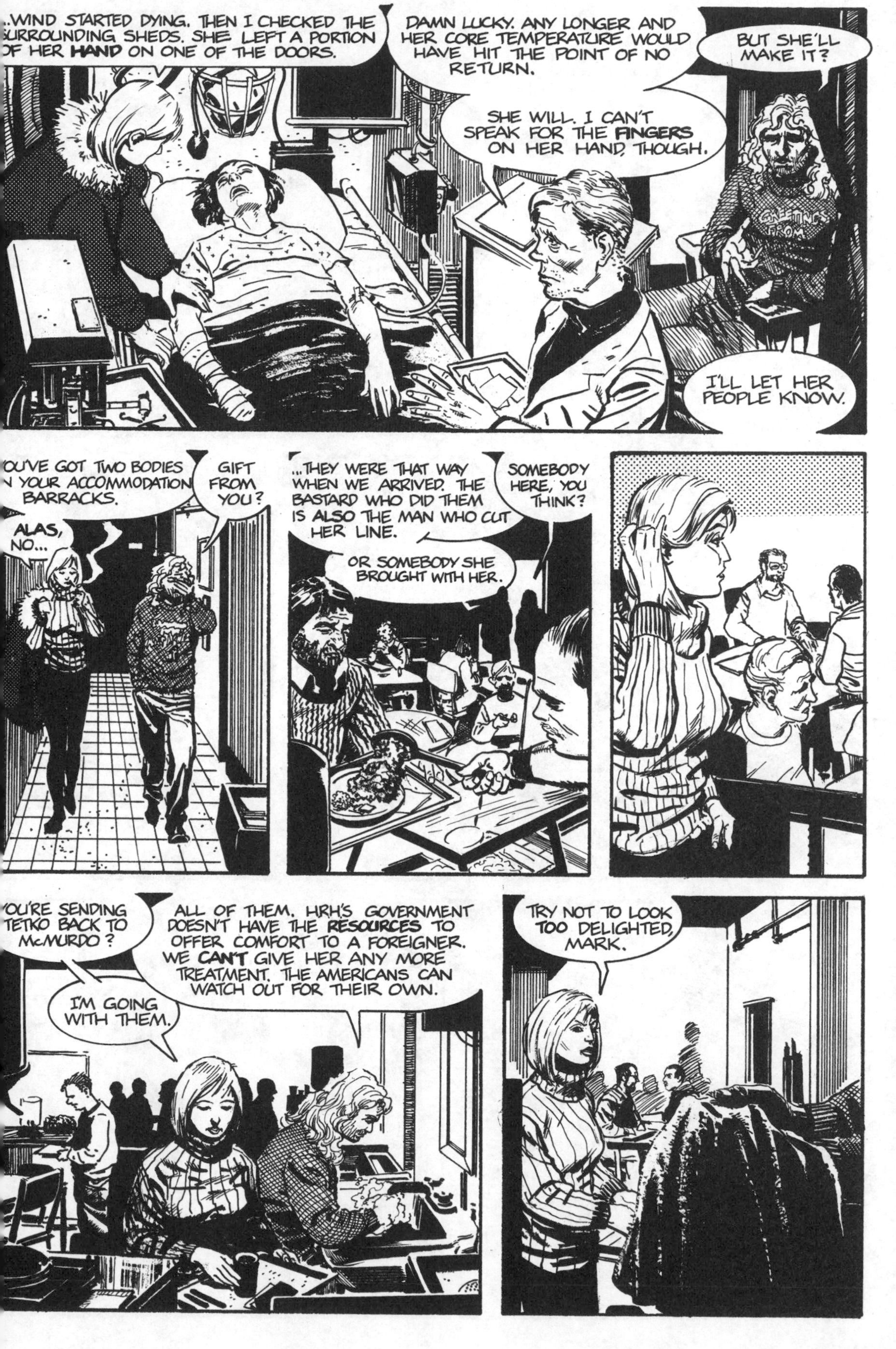
...WIND STARTED DYING. THEN I CHECKED THE SURROUNDING SHEDS. SHE LEFT A PORTION OF HER HAND ON ONE OF THE DOORS.
DAMN LUCKY. ANY LONGER AND HER CORE TEMPERATURE WOULD HAVE HIT THE POINT OF NO RETURN.
BUT SHE'LL MAKE IT?
SHE WILL. I CAN'T SPEAK FOR THE FINGERS ON HER HAND, THOUGH.
I'LL LET HER PEOPLE KNOW.
YOU'VE GOT TWO BODIES IN YOUR ACCOMMODATION BARRACKS.
GIFT FROM YOU?
ALAS, NO...
...THEY WERE THAT WAY WHEN WE ARRIVED. THE BASTARD WHO DID THEM IS ALSO THE MAN WHO CUT HER LINE.
SOMEBODY HERE, YOU THINK?
OR SOMEBODY SHE BROUGHT WITH HER.
YOU'RE SENDING TETKO BACK TO McMURDO?
ALL OF THEM. HRH'S GOVERNMENT DOESN'T HAVE THE RESOURCES TO OFFER COMFORT TO A FOREIGNER. WE CAN'T GIVE HER ANY MORE TREATMENT. THE AMERICANS CAN WATCH OUT FOR THEIR OWN.
I'M GOING WITH THEM.
TRY NOT TO LOOK TOO DELIGHTED, MARK.

Said I was fit to travel. I'm practically warm again.

...DOWN IN TWENTY MINUTES. HOW YOU DOING BACK THERE?

WE'RE FINE.

But I still can't feel my hand.

No, we're not.

We can't be.

HOW YOU FEELING, SLUGGER?

THAWING.

Somebody tried to kill me.

FROSTBITE, BUT WE'LL SEE. SHOULDN'T HAVE TAKEN OFF YOUR GLOVE.

SHE HAD TO OPEN A DOOR, DOCTOR. SHE DIDN'T HAVE A CHOICE.

Wanted me to freeze to death... My body might never have been found.

FUCK.

LOOKS LIKE IT THAWED AND THEN REFROZE, KIDDO.

CARRIE?

Whoever killed Siple and Mooney probably killed Keller, too. Why?

Afraid that they would talk? Or some other reason?

FEEL THAT?

NO.

I NEED YOU TO **LISTEN** TO ME NOW.

GO AHEAD.

WHAT THE FROSTBITE STARTED TO DO ON YOUR FINGERS YOU **FINISHED** WHEN YOU AVULSED THE FLESH WHILE OPENING THE DOOR. THE DAMAGE IS **EXTENSIVE.**

SPIT IT OUT, DOC.

HE'S TELLING YOU YOUR FINGERS ARE DEAD.

IS THAT RIGHT?

THE CELLS FROZE, THAWED, FROZE, AND THAWED AGAIN.

THE FINGERS ARE TURNING **GANGRENOUS** AND IT'LL SPREAD. I'M GOING TO HAVE TO AMPUTATE.

OH.

Amputation is apparently an out-patient procedure. At least on the ice.

Some anesthesia, snip-snip, wrap-wrap, and you're done.

Off with the fingers yesterday morning...

...back to your room the next day...

...back to your life.

...Back to work.

I've got nothing. No suspects. Just a rising body count.

Dammit - keep forgetting.

Nothing. Ten days since Keller was found dead...

...four days since my freeze at Victoria...

...and I've got nothing...

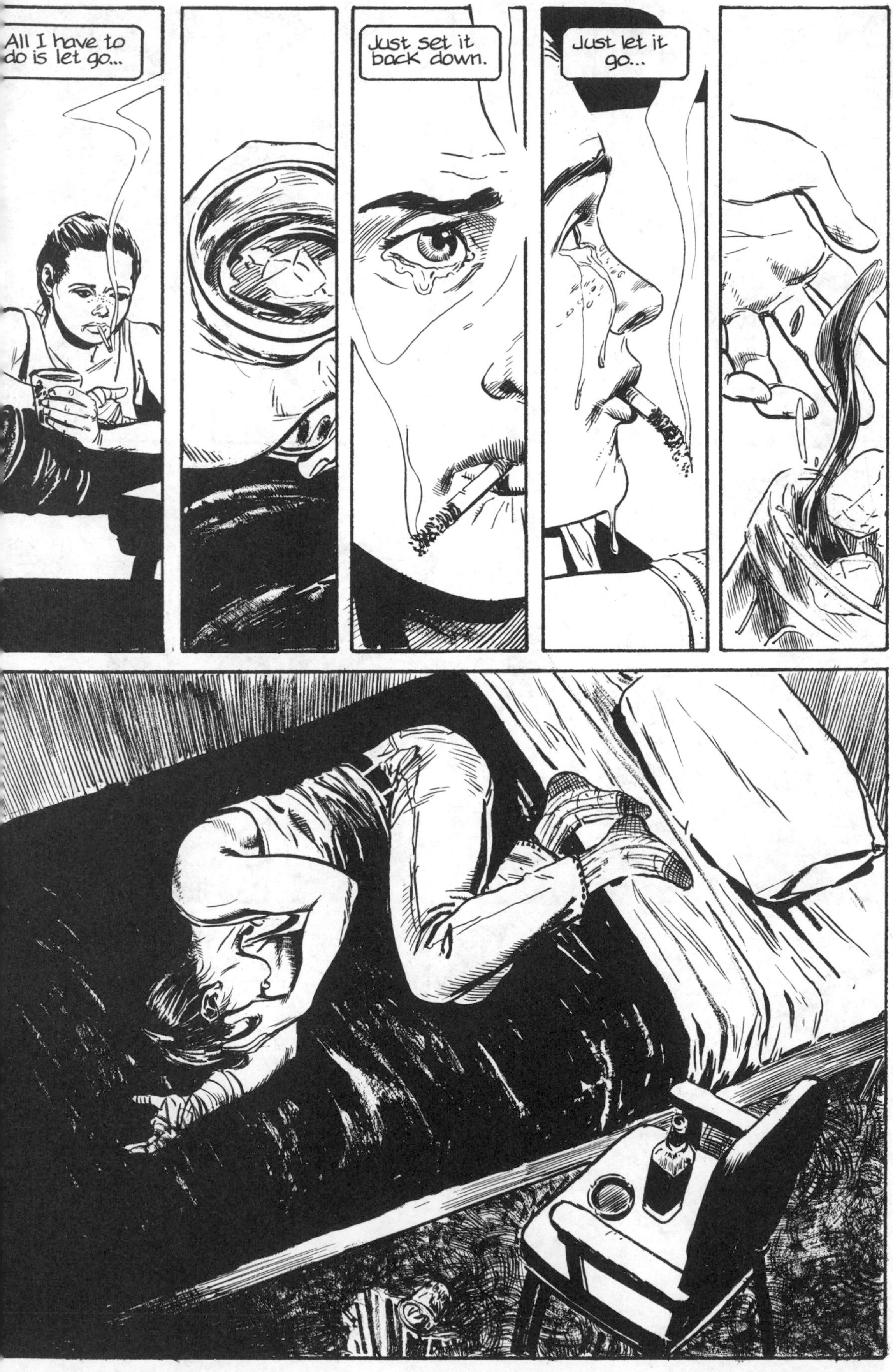
All I have to do is let go...
Just set it back down.
Just let it go...

MARSHAL, IT'S SHARPE, MAY I COME IN?

THINK ITS ONE OF THIS LOT THAT TRIED TO DO US THEN?

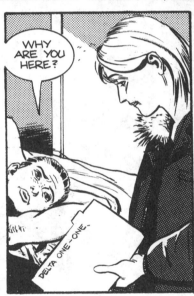

WHY ARE YOU HERE?

DELTA ONE-ONE

I'D THINK YOU'D BE A LITTLE MORE PLEASANT, WHAT WITH MY SAVING YOUR LIFE AND ALL.

HOW'S YOUR HAND?

DIMINISHED.

COULD HAVE BEEN WORSE.

I KNOW. ANSWER MY QUESTION.

I'M HERE TO HELP.

THAT'S SO SWEET.

THIS IS NOT JUST AN AMERICAN PROBLEM, NOW, MARSHAL. SIPLE AN MOONEY WERE ENGLISH. FALLS UNDER MY PURVIEW.

THE BRITISH DON'T HAVE A LAWMAN ON THE ICE.

NO. THAT'S CORRECT.

THEN WHO THE FUCK ARE YOU?

IT'S REALLY NOT RELEVANT.

MY ASS.

I'M THE WOMAN WHO SAVED YOUR LIFE. LET'S LEAVE IT AT *THAT*, SHALL WE?

SNIPK

AS I'VE SAID, I'M HERE TO HELP.

OKAY, HELP.

I'VE GOT A FRIEND AT AMUNDSEN-SCOTT—

LUCKY YOU.

—WHO TELLS ME THAT WESSELHOEFT AND RUBIN ARE ON STATION.

MIGHT BE WORTH TALKING TO.

HOW LONG THEY BEEN THERE?

ARRIVED THREE DAYS AGO...

WESSELHOEFT, J.

RUBIN, B.

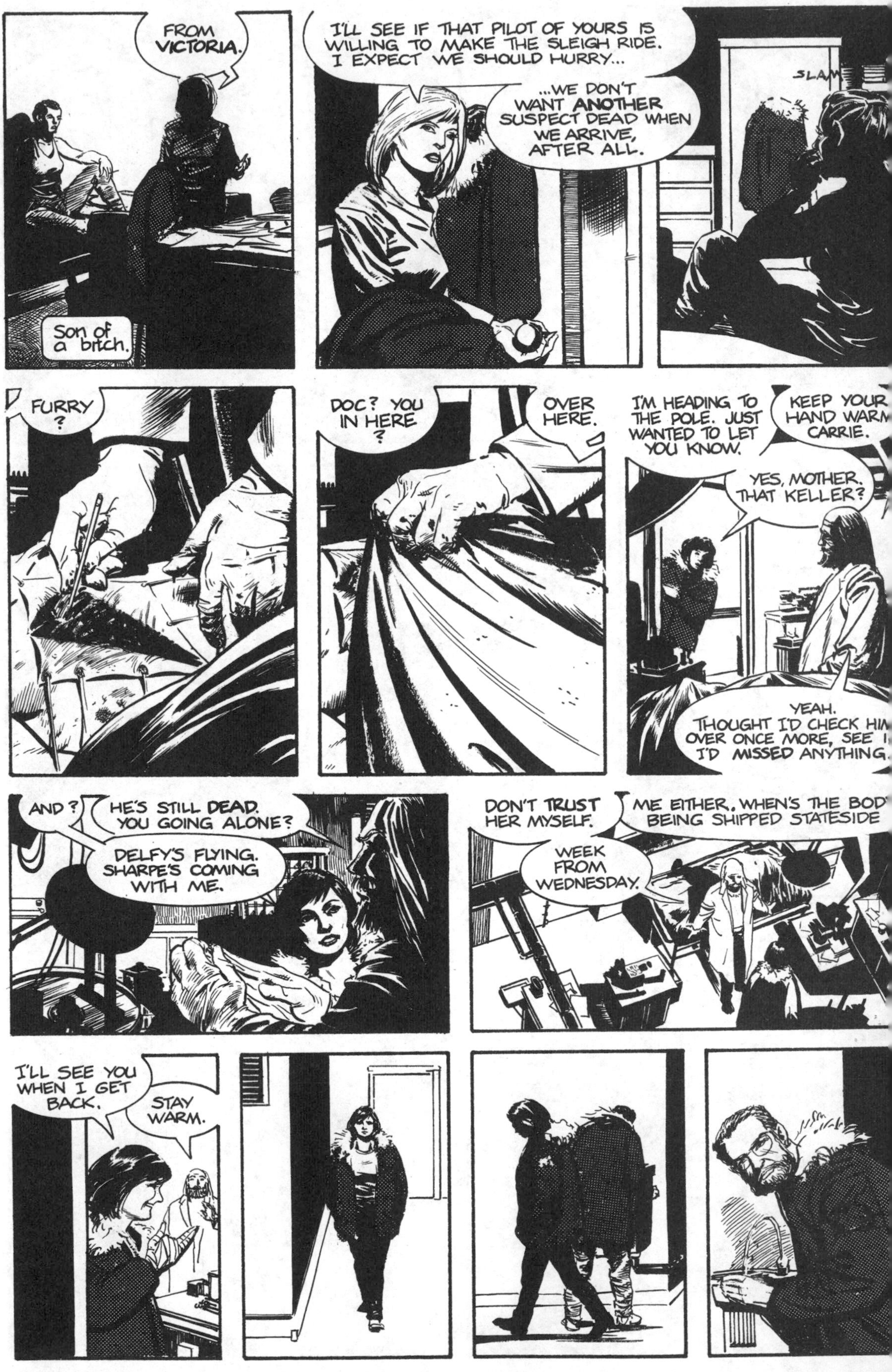
FROM VICTORIA.
Son of a bitch.
I'LL SEE IF THAT PILOT OF YOURS IS WILLING TO MAKE THE SLEIGH RIDE. I EXPECT WE SHOULD HURRY...
...WE DON'T WANT ANOTHER SUSPECT DEAD WHEN WE ARRIVE, AFTER ALL.
SLAM
FURRY?
DOC? YOU IN HERE?
OVER HERE.
I'M HEADING TO THE POLE. JUST WANTED TO LET YOU KNOW.
KEEP YOUR HAND WARM CARRIE.
YES, MOTHER. THAT KELLER?
YEAH. THOUGHT I'D CHECK HIM OVER ONCE MORE, SEE IF I'D MISSED ANYTHING.
AND?
HE'S STILL DEAD. YOU GOING ALONE?
DELFY'S FLYING. SHARPE'S COMING WITH ME.
DON'T TRUST HER MYSELF.
ME EITHER. WHEN'S THE BODY BEING SHIPPED STATESIDE
WEEK FROM WEDNESDAY.
I'LL SEE YOU WHEN I GET BACK.
STAY WARM.

.KELLER'S PRESENCE ?

NSFA. HAD HIS PAPERS. GOT ADDED TO THE TEAM LATE. THAT'S WHY HE WASN'T IN THE FILE.

I WANT AN ARREST.

DO MORE.

GIVE ME A BREAK, BRETT! I'M DOING EVERYTHING I CAN.

ASSHOLE!

MARSHAL?

WHAT?

LIEUTENANT DELFY SAYS WE'RE CLEAR. WEATHER'S GOOD.

WELL? COME ON.

THAT YOUR SUPERIOR YOU WERE CHATTING WITH?

MY BOSS.

HIS NAME IS BRETT?

MARSHAL BRETT McEWAN. WHY?

YOU WERE SAYING HIS NAME WHEN I FOUND YOU IN THE SHED.

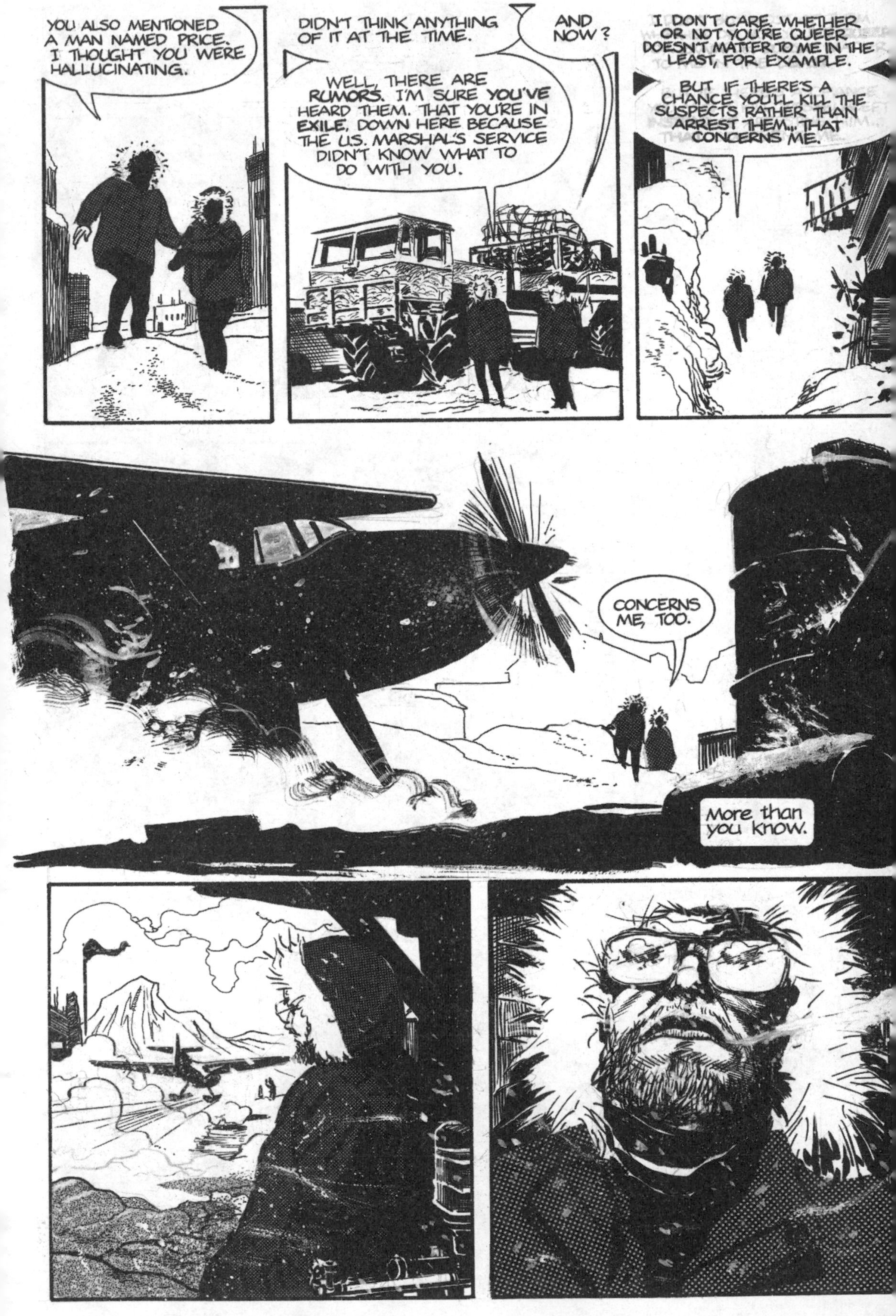
YOU ALSO MENTIONED A MAN NAMED PRICE. I THOUGHT YOU WERE HALLUCINATING.
DIDN'T THINK ANYTHING OF IT AT THE TIME.
AND NOW?
WELL, THERE ARE RUMORS. I'M SURE YOU'VE HEARD THEM. THAT YOU'RE IN EXILE, DOWN HERE BECAUSE THE U.S. MARSHAL'S SERVICE DIDN'T KNOW WHAT TO DO WITH YOU.
I DON'T CARE. WHETHER OR NOT YOU'RE QUEER DOESN'T MATTER TO ME IN THE LEAST, FOR EXAMPLE.
BUT IF THERE'S A CHANCE YOU'LL KILL THE SUSPECTS RATHER THAN ARREST THEM... THAT CONCERNS ME.
CONCERNS ME, TOO.
More than you know.

KEEP THE FREEZER CLOSED!

CLUNGK

WONDERING WHEN YOU'D FIND TIME FOR ME.

LET'S TALK DOC.

Welcome to 90° South. From here you can walk around the world in under a minute.

That's not the real Pole, of course. That's the "Ceremonial Pole" used for publicity shots to be shown to taxpayers back in the world.

The "real" pole is simply a stick.

I prefer the stick.

Twilight here, at least for another couple weeks. Then it goes dark, and the sun won't shine for another three months.

Temperature's about minus 40° F. and that's only one of the polar worries.

See, at the Pole, you're at 9,300 feet above sea level. But because of the atmosphere's thinness and the cold, it feels like 10,500 feet.

So, you have the added bonus of altitude sickness.

I'LL MEET YOU IN THE MESS HALL, MARSHAL. I WANT TO TALK TO MY CONTACT FIRST.

I'LL COME WITH YOU.

AMUNDSEN-SCOTT SOUTH POLE

NO.

SO, WHO IS SHE?

SHE'S A SPOOK.

NOT A SCIENTIST?

NOPE. MAYBE MILITARY INTELLIGENCE.

REMINDS ME OF YOU, KIND OF.

YOU'RE BOTH BITCHY.

YOU CAN'T TELL, BUT I'M GIVING YOU THE FINGER.

GETTING A REFILL. WANT ONE?

SURE.

ALEXANDER KELLER
'78 '28 UNIVERSITY of CHICAGO
Dept. of Geology & Geophysical S/L

# CHAPTER THREE

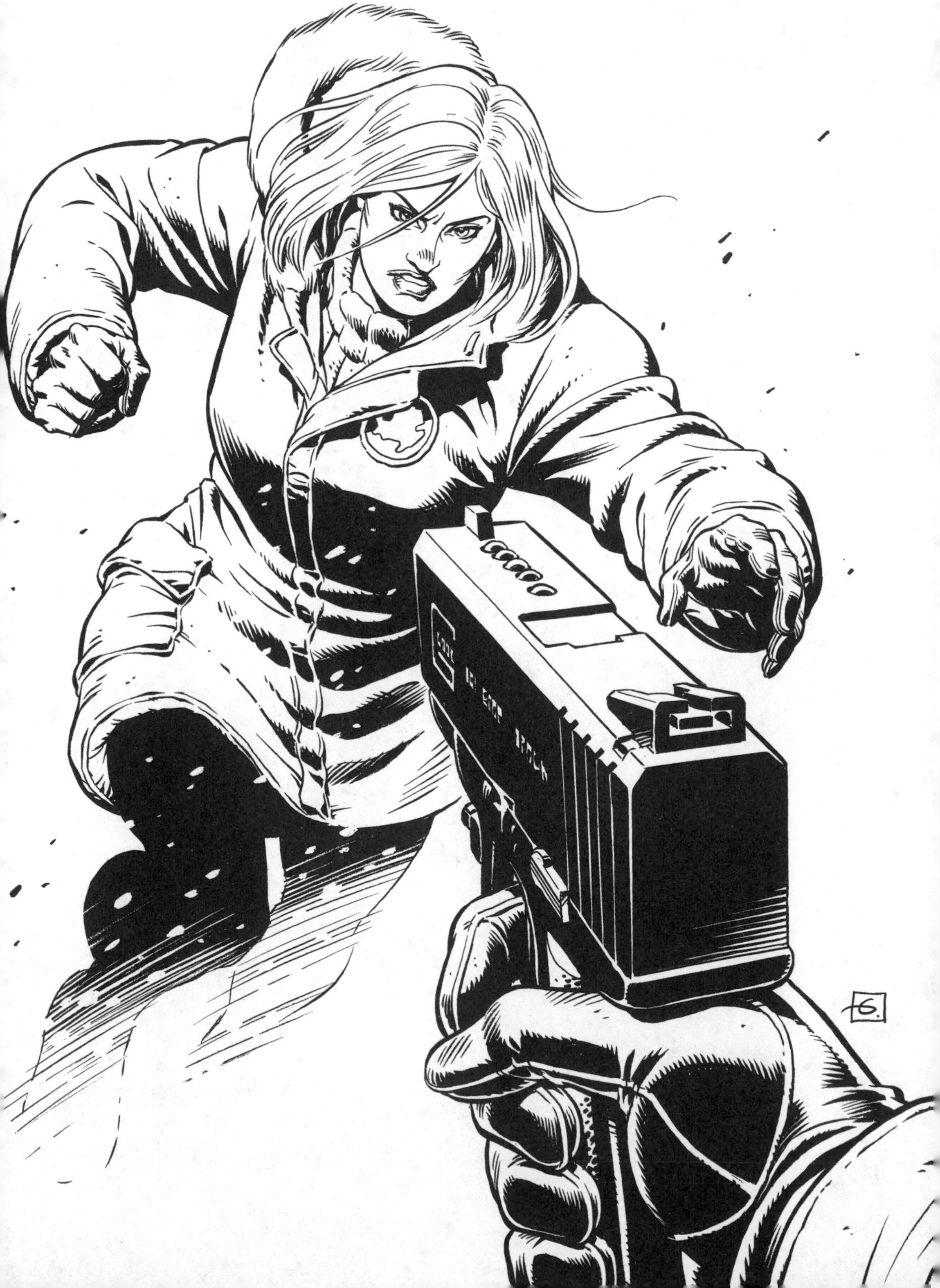

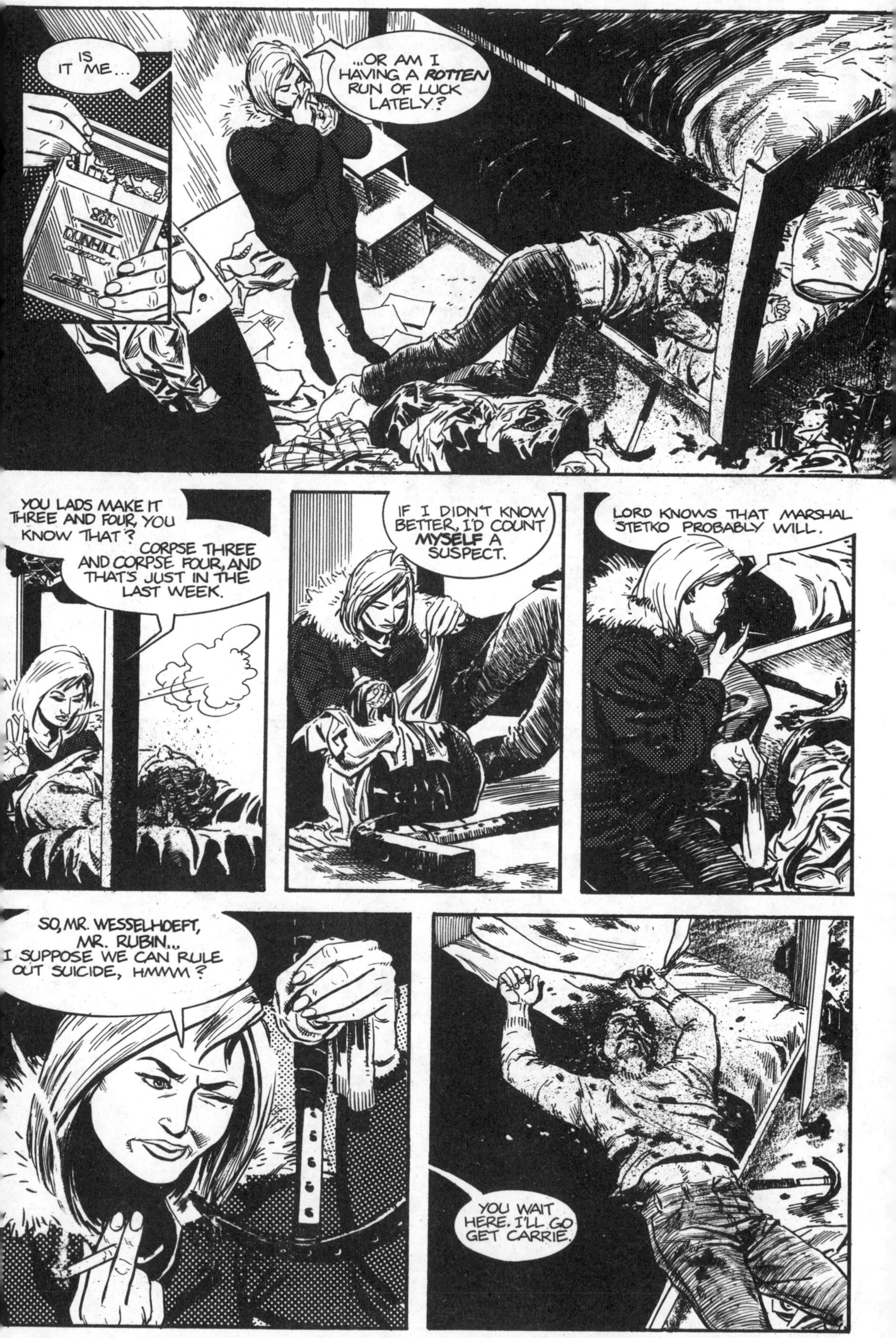
IS IT ME...
...OR AM I HAVING A *ROTTEN* RUN OF LUCK LATELY?
DUNHILL
YOU LADS MAKE IT THREE AND FOUR, YOU KNOW THAT?
CORPSE THREE AND CORPSE FOUR, AND THAT'S JUST IN THE LAST WEEK.
IF I DIDN'T KNOW BETTER, I'D COUNT **MYSELF** A SUSPECT.
LORD KNOWS THAT MARSHAL STETKO PROBABLY WILL.
SO, MR. WESSELHOEFT, MR. RUBIN... I SUPPOSE WE CAN RULE OUT SUICIDE, HMMM?
YOU WAIT HERE. I'LL GO GET CARRIE.

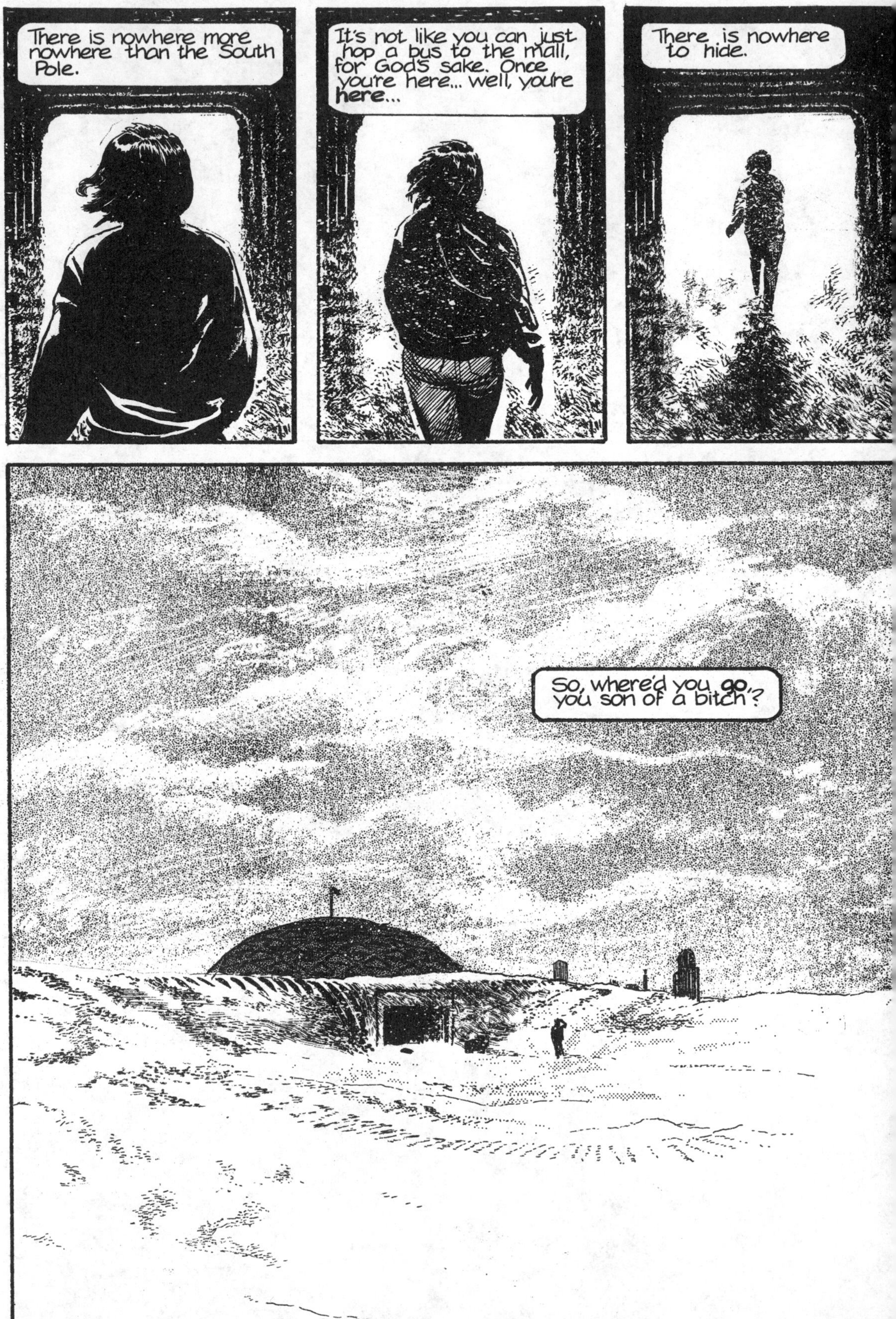
There is nowhere more nowhere than the South Pole.
It's not like you can just hop a bus to the mall, for God's sake. Once you're here... well, you're here...
There is nowhere to hide.
So, where'd you go, you son of a bitch?

MARSHAL? WHAT'S GOING ON? WAS THAT KELLER?

YES.

...BUT HE'S DEAD.

I KNOW.

...I BROUGHT YOU YOUR PARKA...

CARRIE, WE'VE GOT—

NOT NOW.

IT'S RUBIN AND WESSELHOEFT. THEY'VE BEEN MURDERED.

WHAT A SHOCK.

PERHAPS I MISSPOKE... I SAID WESSELHOEF—

KELLER'S ALIVE.

WHAT THE BLOODY HELL'S GOING ON HERE?

S.P.A.M.
South Pole
Area Manager

--TRY KNOCKING FIRST? CHRIST...

CLOSE THE STATION.

EXCUSE ME?

YOU HEARD ME.

GO TO **HELL**. WE'VE GOT A NATIONAL GUARD FLIGHT COMING IN FROM CHRISTCHURCH.

IF YOU THINK I'M PUTTING MY WINTER RESUPPLY IN JEOPARDY BECAUSE SOME BALL-BREAKING **BITCH** BARGES INTO MY OFFICE AND **ORDERS** ME TO, YOU'VE--

FUP.

WHUMP

TELL ME WHAT YOU SEE.

LET GO OF ME!

COME ON, **TELL** ME, WHAT DO YOU SEE?

...IT'S A BADGE...

WHAT **KIND** OF BADGE?

...A MARSHAL'S BADGE...

RIGHT.

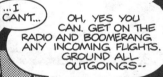

NOW, **CLOSE** THIS STATION AND CLOSE IT FUCKING **NOW,** OR ELSE I'LL **INCARCERATE** YOUR ASS FOR OBSTRUCTION.

...I CAN'T...

OH, YES YOU CAN. GET ON THE RADIO AND BOOMERANG ANY INCOMING FLIGHTS. GROUND ALL OUTGOINGS--

SOME OF THOSE FLIGHTS WILL HAVE PASSED PSR--

IF THEY'VE PASSED POINT OF SAFE RETURN, **DIVERT** THEM. THIS BASE IS CLOSED.

ONCE THAT'S DONE, ASSEMBLE YOUR PEOPLE IN THE DINING HALL.

YOU'VE GOT TWENTY MINUTES.

...PREPARING FOR **WINTEROVER**, SO I'LL TRY TO KEEP THIS BRIEF.

ISAAC WESSELHOEPT AND BATÉS RUBIN WERE FOUND DEAD IN THEIR QUARTERS ROUGHLY AN HOUR AGO. WE BELIEVE THEY WERE KILLED BY ALEX KELLER, WHO IS STILL AT LARGE SOMEWHERE ON STATION.

I AM HEREBY **DEPUTIZING** ALL PRESENT AS AGENTS OF THE UNITED STATES MARSHALS SERVICE. YOU WILL BE BROKEN INTO TEAMS AND ASSIGNED SECTORS OF THE BASE TO SEARCH.

KELLER IS EXTREMELY DANGEROUS. IF YOU LOCATE HIM, NOTIFY YOUR STATION MANAGER, MYSELF, OR MS. SHARPE IMMEDIATELY.

THAT'S IT. GO TO IT.

This couldn't have come at a **worse** time for them.

The pole is **inaccessible** from mid-February to mid-October. No flights in or out.

The sky goes dark and the temperature matches that of equatorial **Mars**...

Finding a fugitive is **low** on their list of priorities.

Especially one presumed dead...

...how'd we miss that, huh? His prints came back—

CARRIE?

DELFY AND I ARE GOING TO CHECK OUTSIDE.

I'LL JOIN YOU.

BEST IF YOU DON'T. BAD FOR YOUR HAND, I'D THINK.

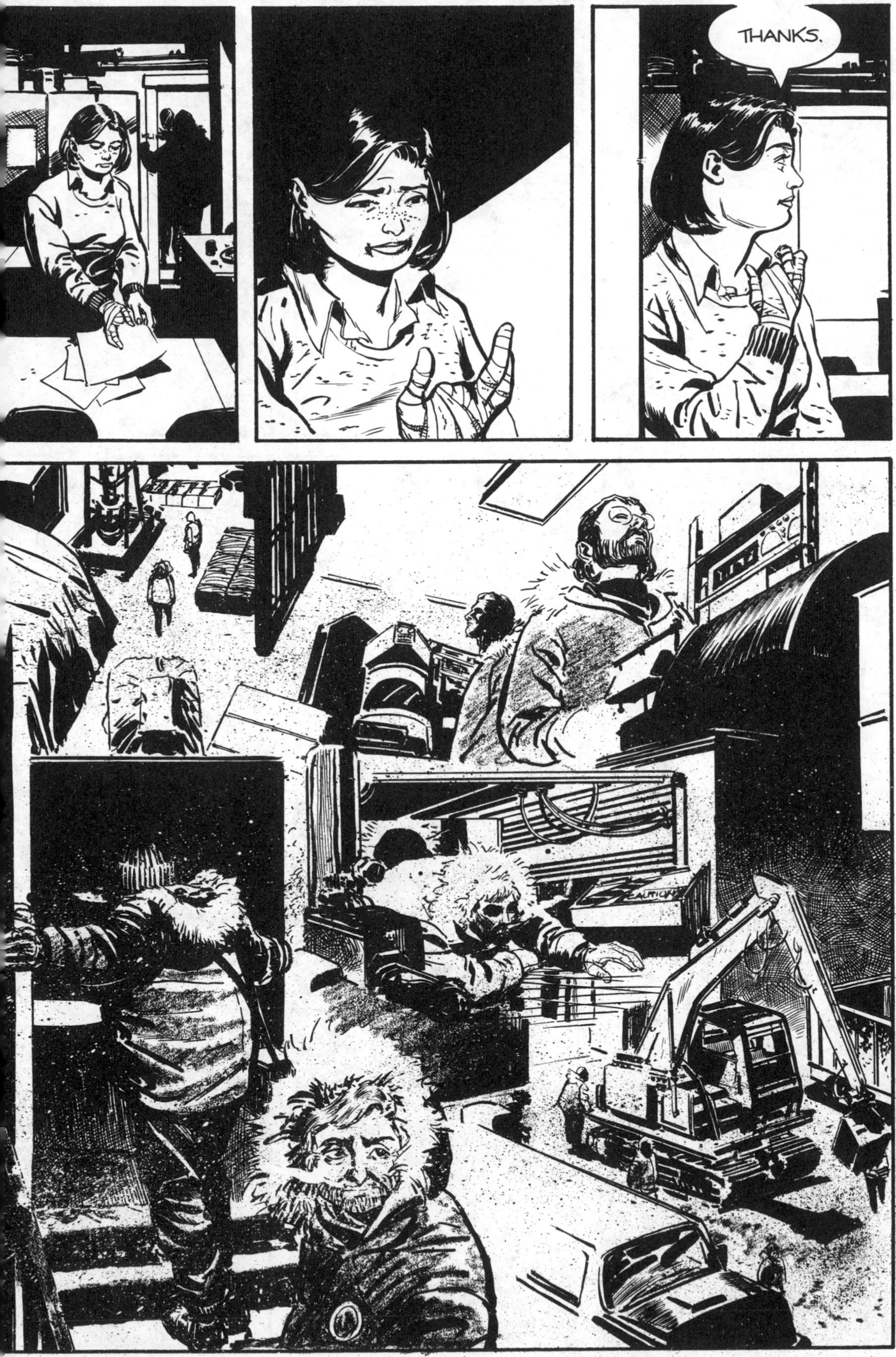
THANKS.

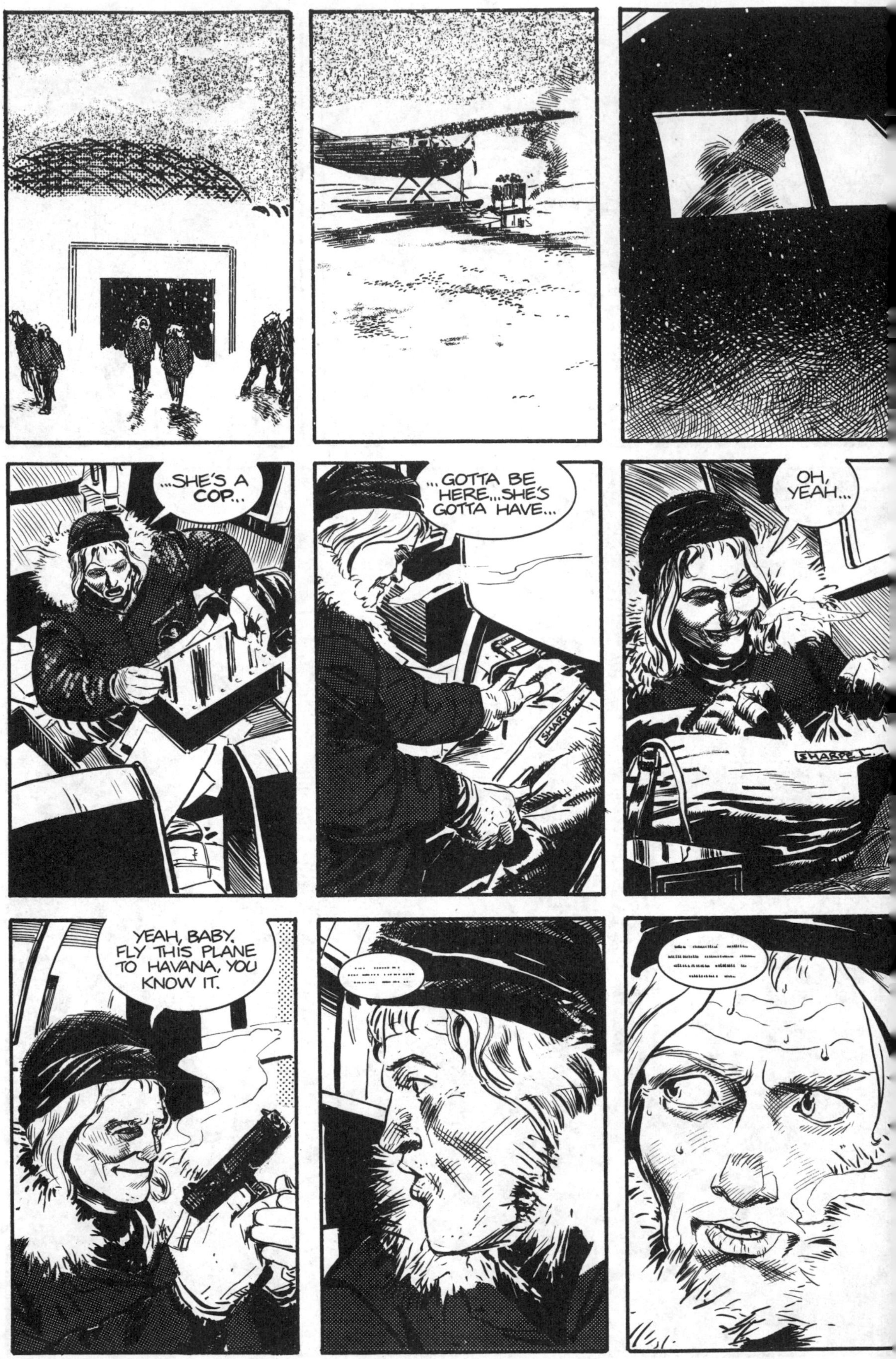
...SHE'S A COP...
...GOTTA BE HERE...SHE'S GOTTA HAVE...
SHARPE, L.
OH, YEAH...
SHARPE, L.
YEAH, BABY. FLY THIS PLANE TO HAVANA, YOU KNOW IT.

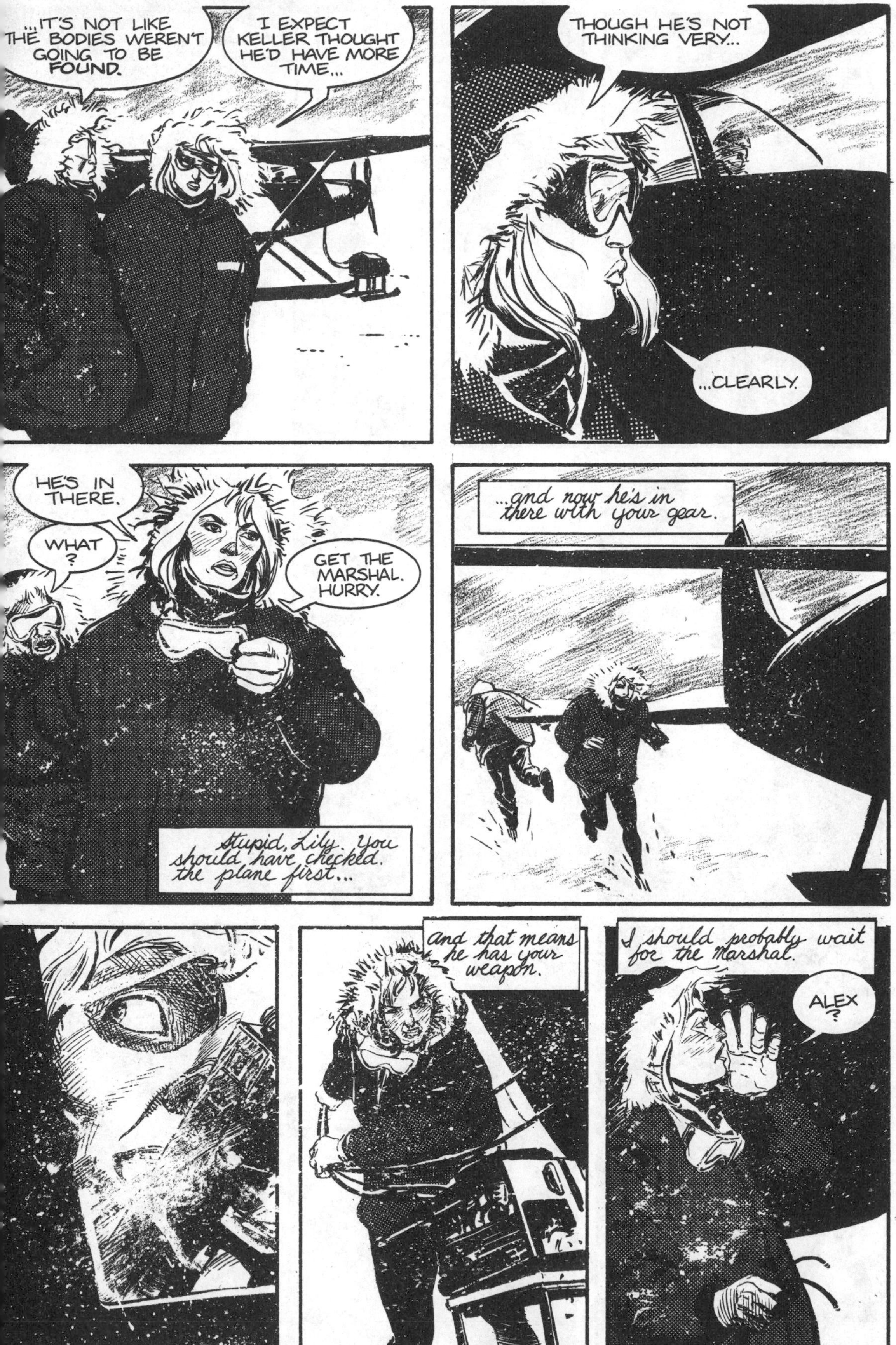
...IT'S NOT LIKE THE BODIES WEREN'T GOING TO BE FOUND.
I EXPECT KELLER THOUGHT HE'D HAVE MORE TIME...
THOUGH HE'S NOT THINKING VERY...
...CLEARLY.
HE'S IN THERE.
WHAT?
GET THE MARSHAL. HURRY.
Stupid, Lily. You should have checked the plane first...
...and now he's in there with your gear.
and that means he has your weapon.
I should probably wait for the Marshal.
ALEX?

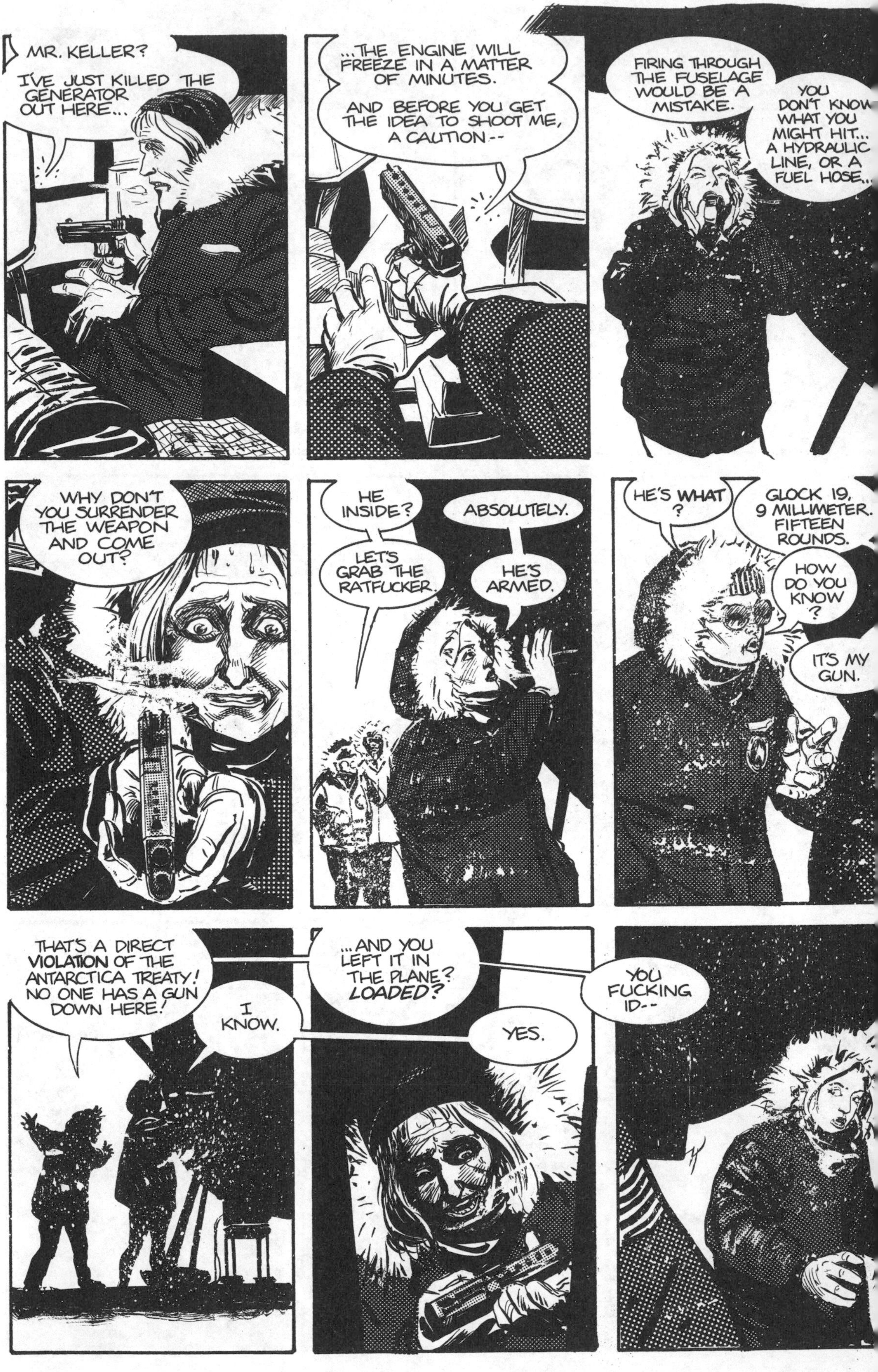
MR. KELLER?
I'VE JUST KILLED THE GENERATOR OUT HERE...
...THE ENGINE WILL FREEZE IN A MATTER OF MINUTES.
AND BEFORE YOU GET THE IDEA TO SHOOT ME, A CAUTION--
FIRING THROUGH THE FUSELAGE WOULD BE A MISTAKE.
YOU DON'T KNOW WHAT YOU MIGHT HIT... A HYDRAULIC LINE, OR A FUEL HOSE...
WHY DON'T YOU SURRENDER THE WEAPON AND COME OUT?
HE INSIDE?
ABSOLUTELY.
LET'S GRAB THE RATFUCKER.
HE'S ARMED.
HE'S WHAT?
GLOCK 19, 9 MILLIMETER. FIFTEEN ROUNDS.
HOW DO YOU KNOW?
IT'S MY GUN.
THAT'S A DIRECT VIOLATION OF THE ANTARCTICA TREATY! NO ONE HAS A GUN DOWN HERE!
I KNOW.
...AND YOU LEFT IT IN THE PLANE? LOADED?
YES.
YOU FUCKING ID--

He's nothing if not predictable...

...and he certainly isn't trying anything new...

I'M THE ONLY ONE WITH A GUN, HUH? SUCKS FOR YOU GUYS.

That's a good lad...

...that's *just what* I want.

NOW, LOO, CLIMB ON IN AND START HER UP. OR ELSE I SPRAY THE MARSHAL'S BRAINS ALL OVER THE POLAR PLATEAU.

JESUS, ALEX! YOU'R'

AND WHERE WILL YOU GO, ALEX?

Good, Lily, good. Get him talking.

I'VE GOT A HOSTAGE. THAT'LL DO.

IT MIGHT GET YOU TO McMURDO, BUT YOU'LL NEED MORE THAN JUST HER TO MAKE IT TO CHRISTCHURCH.

LISTEN TO HER, ALEX.

SHUT UP!

Oh, my God...

...he's going to do it.

He already tried to kill me once.

WE DON'T KNOW THAT.

WE ALL KNOW YOU WON'T DO IT.

HE DOESN'T HAVE IT IN HIM.

All right...

...let's see what you're made of..

I'LL KILL HER!

YOU DON'T HAVE THE BALLS.

...Jesus, Lily, you're going to get me shot...

STOP WASTING OUR TIME, BOY.

Come on, boy, pull the trigger, you can...

Have a plan, please have a...

...do it.

krk

Snap

...plan!

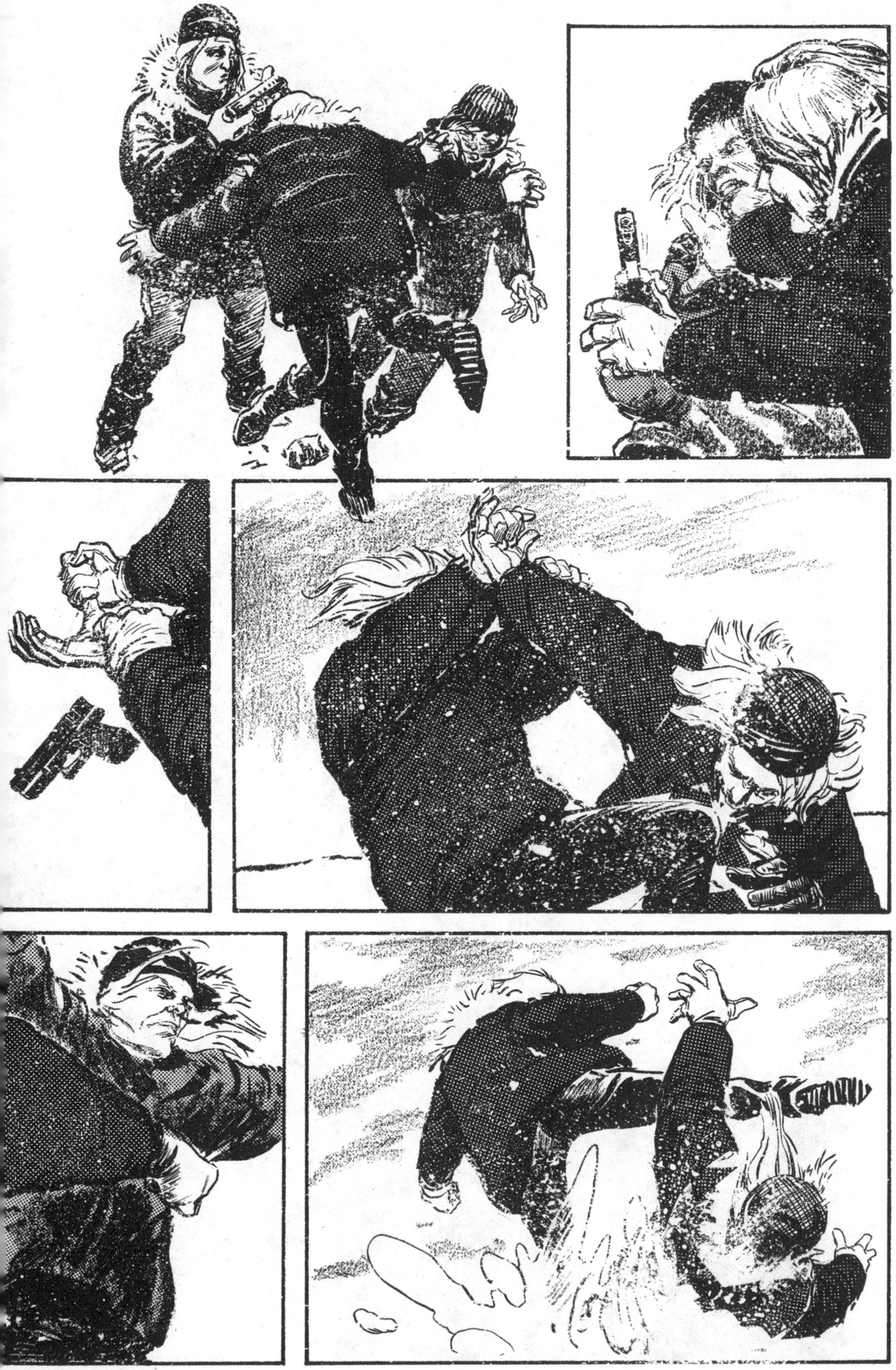

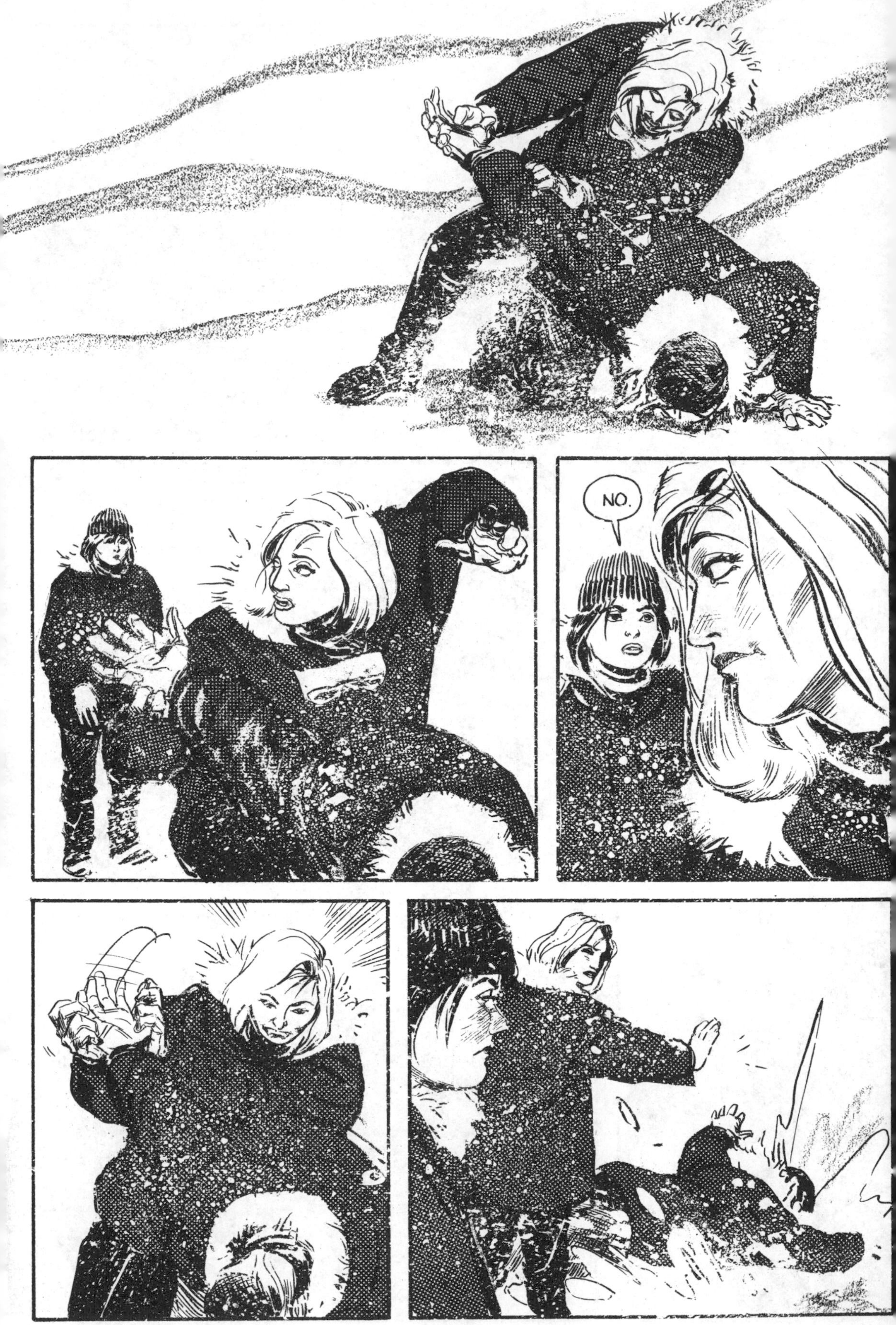
NO.

I'M... UH... WHAT JUST HAPPENED?

THE WEATHER, LIEUTENANT. FROZE THE COMPONENTS OF THE GUN. THE TRIGGER'S SHATTERED.

YOU KNEW THE TRIGGER WOULD BREAK?

OR THE FIRING PIN. ONE OR THE OTHER WAS CERTAIN TO SHATTER FROM THE COLD.

NNGK.

BUT YOU COULDN'T BE SURE.

NO, I COULDN'T BE SURE, LIEUTENANT.

YOU'VE GOT BRASS OVARIES LILY.

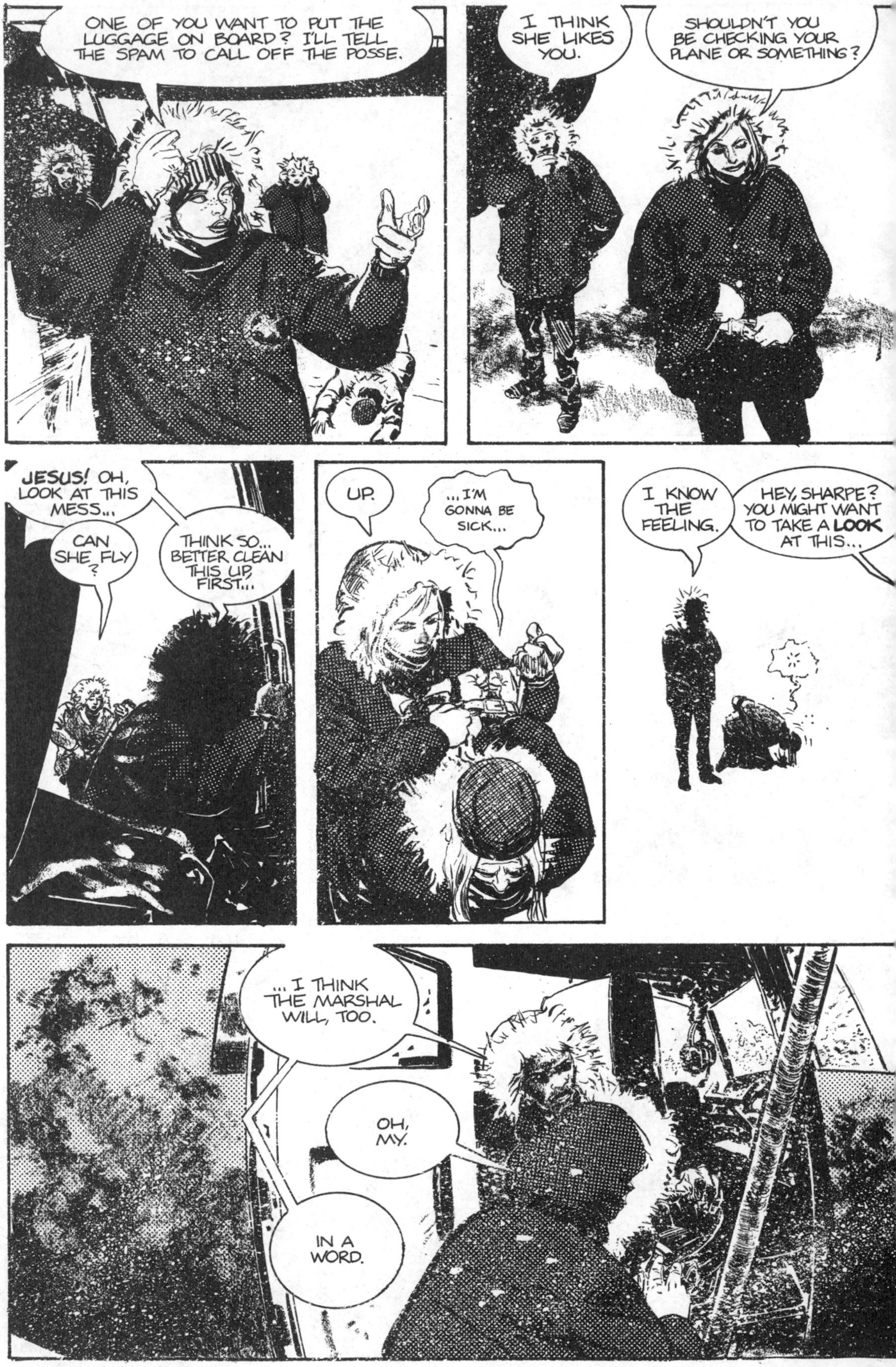
ONE OF YOU WANT TO PUT THE LUGGAGE ON BOARD? I'LL TELL THE SPAM TO CALL OFF THE POSSE.
I THINK SHE LIKES YOU.
SHOULDN'T YOU BE CHECKING YOUR PLANE OR SOMETHING?
JESUS! OH, LOOK AT THIS MESS...
CAN SHE FLY?
THINK SO... BETTER CLEAN THIS UP FIRST...
UP.
...I'M GONNA BE SICK...
I KNOW THE FEELING.
HEY, SHARPE? YOU MIGHT WANT TO TAKE A LOOK AT THIS...
...I THINK THE MARSHAL WILL, TOO.
OH, MY.
IN A WORD.

HEY! YANKEE FAGGOT!

HEY, YOU POME FUCK

SAW YOU LAND, MATE. HOW'D THE SLEIGH RIDE TREAT YOU?

SOME WILD SHIT AT THE POLE, MAN.

YOU KNOW WHAT'S GOING ON?

THE MARSHAL'S GETTING AN IDEA...

SHE GOT HER MAN.

A TIME-HONORED MOTIVE, MY FRIEND...

NO SHIT? WHY'D HE DO IT?

...**GREED**. LEAST, THAT'S HOW IT LOOKS.

HOW HEAVY DID YOU SAY THEY ARE?

...TEN, MAYBE FIFTEEN POUNDS.

TEN POUNDS EACH, LOOKS LIKE **SOLID** GOLD BEST THAT WE CAN TELL.

WHAT'S THAT WORTH?

ALL OF THEM TOGETHER? AROUND A HUNDRED-SIXTY GRAND.

AND YOU SAY YOU'VE ARRESTED **KELLER**? THE GUY YOU THOUGHT WAS MURDERED?

YOUR PEOPLE RAN THE PRINTS, MARSHAL. IT WAS **YOU** WHO FAXED ME THE I.D.

DON'T PUT A BITCH ON, CARRIE. SOMEONE OBVIOUSLY MADE A MISTAKE.

NO KIDDING. FIGURE THE FIRST BODY WE FOUND WAS THE OTHER AMERICAN ON THE TEAM, WEISS. HE'S THE ONLY ONE NOT ACCOUNTED FOR AS OF NOW.

SOMEONE GOT HIM OFF THE ICE. SOMEONE HELPED HIM MOVE FROM BASE TO BASE.

YOU'VE GOT THE ARREST. THAT'LL DO. DON'T GO NEAR THE PRISONER.

I DON'T

**NO**, DEPUTY! YOU INTERROGATE KELLER, YOU'LL GET THE CASE TOSSED ON A TECHNICALITY. DUE PROCESS, REMEMBER? SOMEBODY'LL COME DOWN TO GET HIM...

...DON'T GO NEAR HIM. **YOUR** INVESTIGATION IS FINISHED. LET IT BE.

CHK

YOU THINK KELLER KILLED ALL FOUR OF THEM?

WHAT NOW?

YOU'RE NOT GOING WHERE I THINK YOU'RE GOING.

WHERE DO YOU THINK I'M GOING?

DON'T. YOU'LL GET THE CASE TOSSED, YOU'LL GET REPRIMANDED, OR WORSE.

I'M NOT ASKING YOU TO HELP ME.

YOU'RE GOING TO LAND YOURSELF IN A WORLD OF TROUBLE WITH McEWAN.

I DON'T CARE. I WANT ANSWERS.

— HOW KELLER GOT OFF THE ICE. WHERE THEIR GEAR WENT, WHO FLEW THEM...

...AND WHY. I WANT TO KNOW A WHOLE LOT OF WHY. IN FACT, I'VE GOT WHY COMING OUT MY EARS — HOLD ON—

KNOCK IT OFF

POP

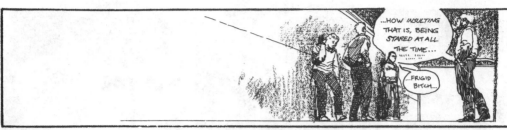

...HOW INSULTING THAT IS, BEING STARED AT ALL THE TIME...

...FRIGID BITCH...

...WAS I SAYING?

YOU WERE LISTING WHYS.

RIGHT. WHY, FOR INSTANCE...

...IS A BRITISH SPY CONCERNED WITH MY INVESTIGATION?

YOU MEAN, ME?

ON THE NOSE.

I'LL FIND OUT SOONER OR LATER, LILY.

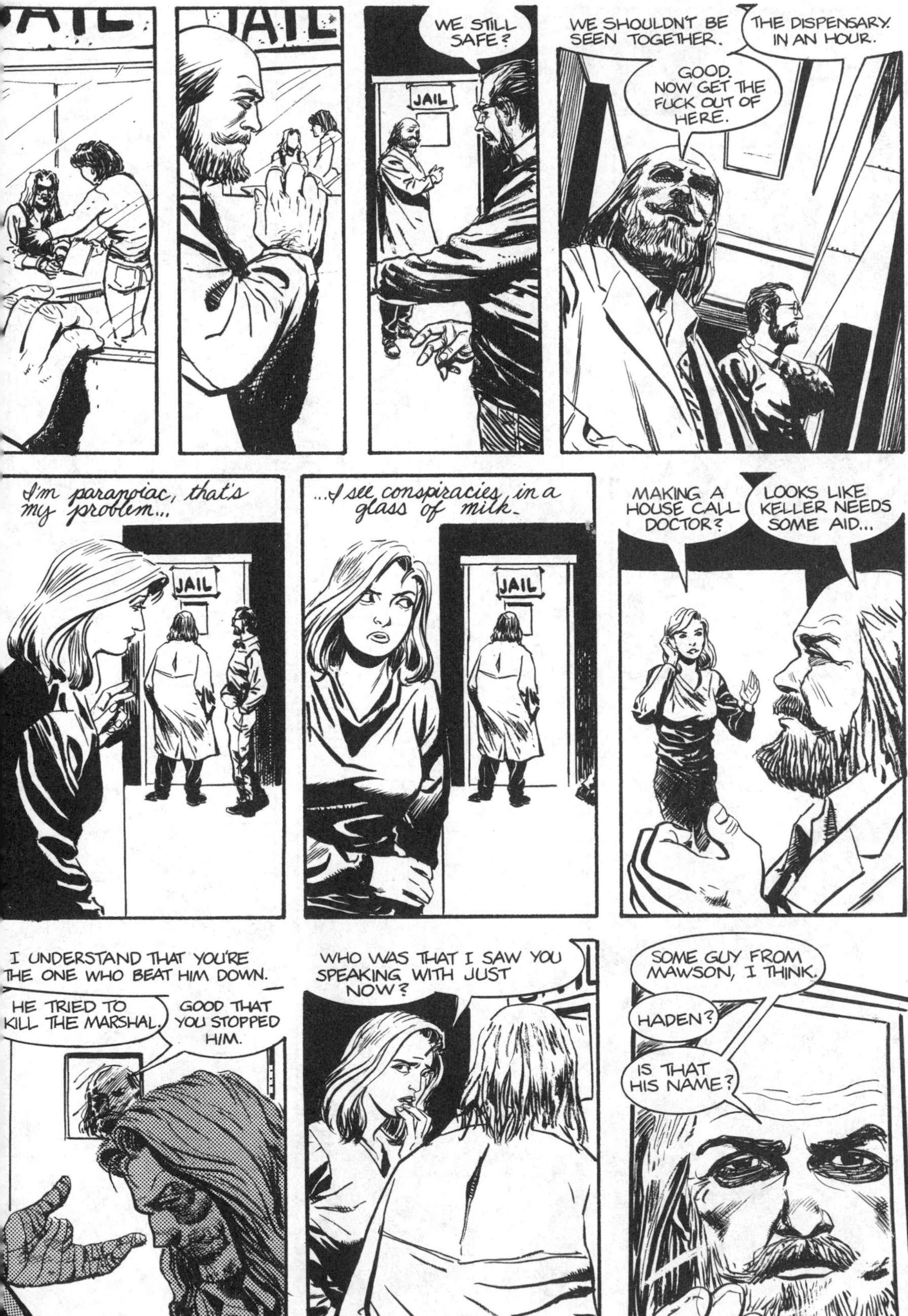
WE STILL SAFE?
WE SHOULDN'T BE SEEN TOGETHER.
THE DISPENSARY. IN AN HOUR.
GOOD. NOW GET THE FUCK OUT OF HERE.
I'm paranoiac, that's my problem...
...I see conspiracies in a glass of milk.
MAKING A HOUSE CALL DOCTOR?
LOOKS LIKE KELLER NEEDS SOME AID...
I UNDERSTAND THAT YOU'RE THE ONE WHO BEAT HIM DOWN.
HE TRIED TO KILL THE MARSHAL.
GOOD THAT YOU STOPPED HIM.
WHO WAS THAT I SAW YOU SPEAKING WITH JUST NOW?
SOME GUY FROM MAWSON, I THINK.
HADEN?
IS THAT HIS NAME?

ISN'T HE A PILO...

...SMUG BASTARD!

CAN I EXAMINE HIM?

HE SAYS ANYTHING TO YOU, I WANT TO KNOW.

WHERE CAN I FIND YOU?

IN MY QUARTERS.

...paranoiac, like I said.

...COMING OR WHAT?

--STATION MANAGER SAYS HE CAN BERTH ME IN A DORM TONIGHT.

YOU'RE NOT HEADING BACK TO VICTORIA?

NOT UNTIL WE FIND THE ACCOMPLICE.

DELFY FLEW KELLER AND RUBIN INTO STATION ALMOS THREE WEEKS BEFORE THE CAMP DISAPPEARED.

I DON'T THINK...

NEITHER DO I. DELFY'S CLEAN.

MUST BE ANOTHER PILOT, THEN...

...ONE KELLER RECRUITED. ANY IDEA HOW LONG IT TAKES TO DRILL THAT MANY HOLES?

QUITE A WHILE, I'D IMAGINE-- ESPECIALLY CONSIDERING HOW FAR ONE MUST GO TO ACTUALLY HIT EARTH.

IF EVEN *HALF* OF THOSE YIELDED GOLD...

...IT'D BE MORE THAN ENOUGH TO *BUY* ANY HELP KELLER REQUIRED.

BUY HIMSELF SOMEONE HERE, AT McMURDO.

THIS WAS *ALL* PLANNED.

NOT WELL, IT WOULD SEEM.

IT WAS *PROBABLY* A GOOD PLAN AT THE *START.* BUT IT WENT WRONG ABOUT THE TIME I WENT TO VICTORIA AND RAN INTO YOU...

WE CHECK THE LOGS, FIND WHO WAS HERE WHEN DELFY BROUGHT THEM IN, CHECK THOSE NAMES AGAINST CURRENT POPULATION.

YOU THINK THEIR ACCOMPLICE LOGGED HIS ARRIVAL?

THAT'S MY HOPE

THAT'S GOING TO BE A LOT OF NAMES.

TRUE. BUT HOW MANY OF THOSE NAMES...

"...ARE REGISTERED PILOTS?"

WERE YOU SEEN?

NO, I MADE SURE.

BOUGHT DELFY A FEW DRINKS, GOT HIM TALKING. THE MARSHAL FOUND THE STICKS KELLER TOOK OFF WESSELHOEFT AND RUBIN.

HOW MANY?

SIXTEEN.

HE DIDN'T GET SUSPICIOUS?

DELFY? NAH. HE'S THE TRUSTIN' SORT. THINKS WE'RE MATES.

SHARPE SAW YOU TALKING TO ME EARLIER.

DID SHE HEAR US?

IF SHE'S TOLD THE MARSHAL, WE'RE FUCKED.

NO. SHE KNOWS ABOUT YOU THOUGH... THAT YOU'RE A PILOT.

CARRIE HASN'T BEEN TO SEE ME... SO I DOUBT SHARPE'S TOLD HER ANYTHING, YET.

OR SHE'S WAITING FOR MORE EVIDENCE. OR MAYBE'LL RUN AT KELLER AGAIN, AND THIS TIME HE COULD GO TITS UP ON US...

WE CAN'T LET HER...

I WON'T LET YOU TOUCH HER HADEN!

DON'T GET SENTIMENTAL.

I SAID NO!

NO MORE BODIES, HADEN. THIS ISN'T WHAT I SIGNED ON FOR.

RELAX, DOC. IF SHARPE'S KEPT QUIET, SHE'S THE ONLY ONE WE HAVE TO WORRY ABOUT--

"...YOU **FIND** OUT. I'LL DO THE REST."

FURRY! SOCIAL OR BUSINESS?

BIT OF BOTH.

"...DIDN'T MEAN TO INTERRUPT.

NAH, WE'RE JUST TRYING TO FILL IN SOME BLANKS.

DOCTOR.

IS THAT BOTTLE FOR SHOW OR ARE YOU GOING TO POUR?

REMEMBER THE GUY WITH THE CLAW HAMMER?

OH, MY GOD!

THIS WOULD'VE BEEN THREE, FOUR YEARS AGO- HOLD STILL-SOME MECHO IN THE MOTOR POOL STARTED CHASING EVERYONE IN THE GARAGE WITH A CLAW HAMMER.

PUT TWO PEOPLE IN THE DISPENSARY.

THE MARSHAL HERE, SHE **WALTZES** INTO THE V.M.F. LIKE SHE'S SOME COWBOY OR SOMETHING.

I AM **NOT** A COWBOY.

AND SHE **ORDERS** THIS GUY TO DROP THE HAMMER.

AND?

AND OF COURSE HE SAYS "NO."

ACTUALLY, HE SAID "EAT ME, BITCH."

-STOMACH, I WAS AIMING FOR HIS STOMACH-

SO CARRIE SHRUGS, STEPS FORWARD, AND KICKS HIM IN THE GNADS.

GUY DOUBLES OVER, LOSES THE HAMMER...

...AND **THAT'S** HOW CARRIE INTRODUCED HERSELF TO McMURDO STATION.

BRAVO!

THANK YOU. IT WAS NOTHING.

AFTER THAT, NO ONE DARED FUCK WITH THE MARSHAL.

I AM SERIOUSLY GOING TO MISS YOU WHEN YOU GO, FURRY.

I'M GOING TO MISS YOU, TOO.

YOU PACKED?

YOU'RE LEAVING?

TOMORROW. LAST FLIGHT OUT.

HIS TOUR'S UP. THEY THINK HIS OLD ANTARCTIC EXPLORER ASS HAS GOTTEN TOO OLD AND TOO COLD...

THEY'LL COME FOR YOU TOO SOMEDAY. DRAG YOU OFF THE ICE KICKING AND SCREAMING...

NO WAY. I'M NEVER GOING BACK. I'LL DIE HERE, AN OAE. WHOSE ASHES GET SCATTERED OVER THE POLE.

THEY WON'T GIVE YOU THE OPTION.

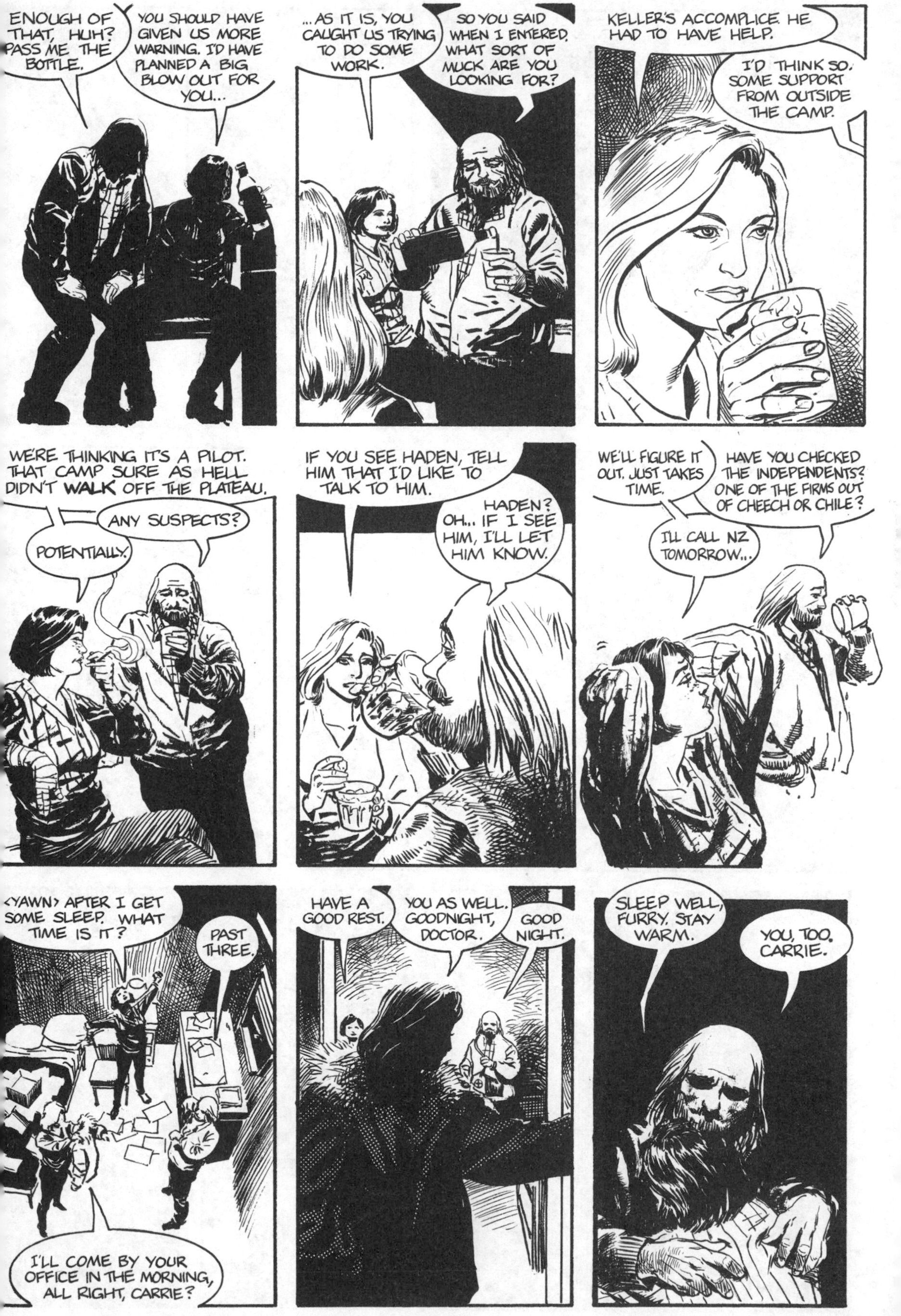
ENOUGH OF THAT, HUH? PASS ME THE BOTTLE.
YOU SHOULD HAVE GIVEN US MORE WARNING. I'D HAVE PLANNED A BIG BLOW OUT FOR YOU...
...AS IT IS, YOU CAUGHT US TRYING TO DO SOME WORK.
SO YOU SAID WHEN I ENTERED. WHAT SORT OF MUCK ARE YOU LOOKING FOR?
KELLER'S ACCOMPLICE. HE HAD TO HAVE HELP.
I'D THINK SO. SOME SUPPORT FROM OUTSIDE THE CAMP.
WE'RE THINKING IT'S A PILOT. THAT CAMP SURE AS HELL DIDN'T WALK OFF THE PLATEAU.
ANY SUSPECTS?
POTENTIALLY.
IF YOU SEE HADEN, TELL HIM THAT I'D LIKE TO TALK TO HIM.
HADEN? OH... IF I SEE HIM, I'LL LET HIM KNOW.
WE'LL FIGURE IT OUT. JUST TAKES TIME.
HAVE YOU CHECKED THE INDEPENDENTS? ONE OF THE FIRMS OUT OF CHEECH OR CHILE?
I'LL CALL NZ TOMORROW...
<YAWN> AFTER I GET SOME SLEEP. WHAT TIME IS IT?
PAST THREE.
I'LL COME BY YOUR OFFICE IN THE MORNING, ALL RIGHT, CARRIE?
HAVE A GOOD REST.
YOU AS WELL. GOODNIGHT, DOCTOR.
GOOD NIGHT.
SLEEP WELL, FURRY. STAY WARM.
YOU, TOO. CARRIE.

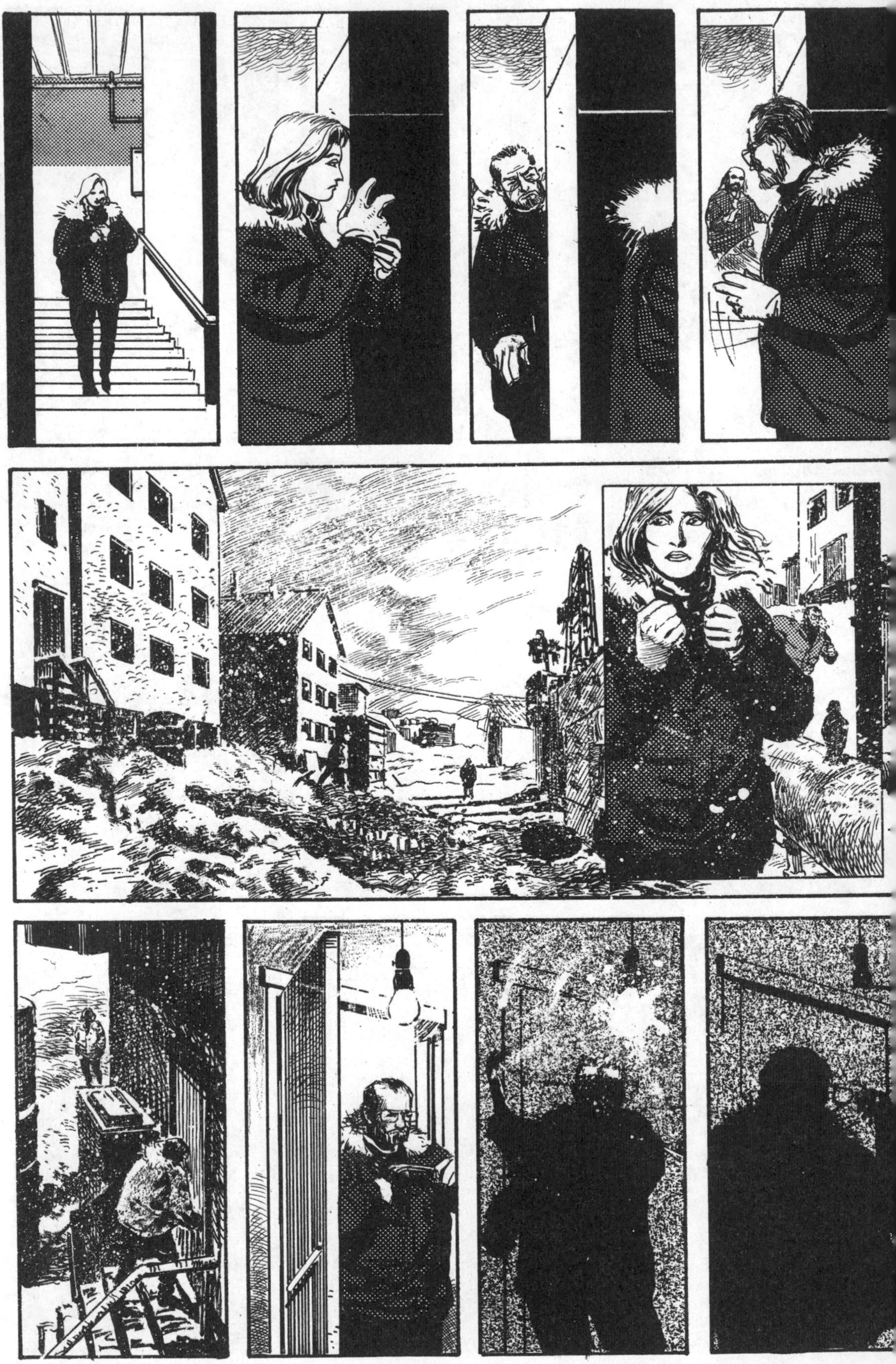

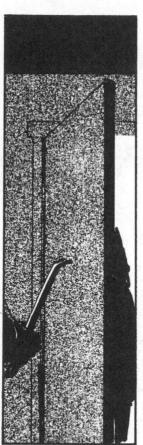

Oh, bloody motherfucking he—

TAK

Is it me...

...or am I having a rotten run of luck lately?...

# CHAPTER FOUR

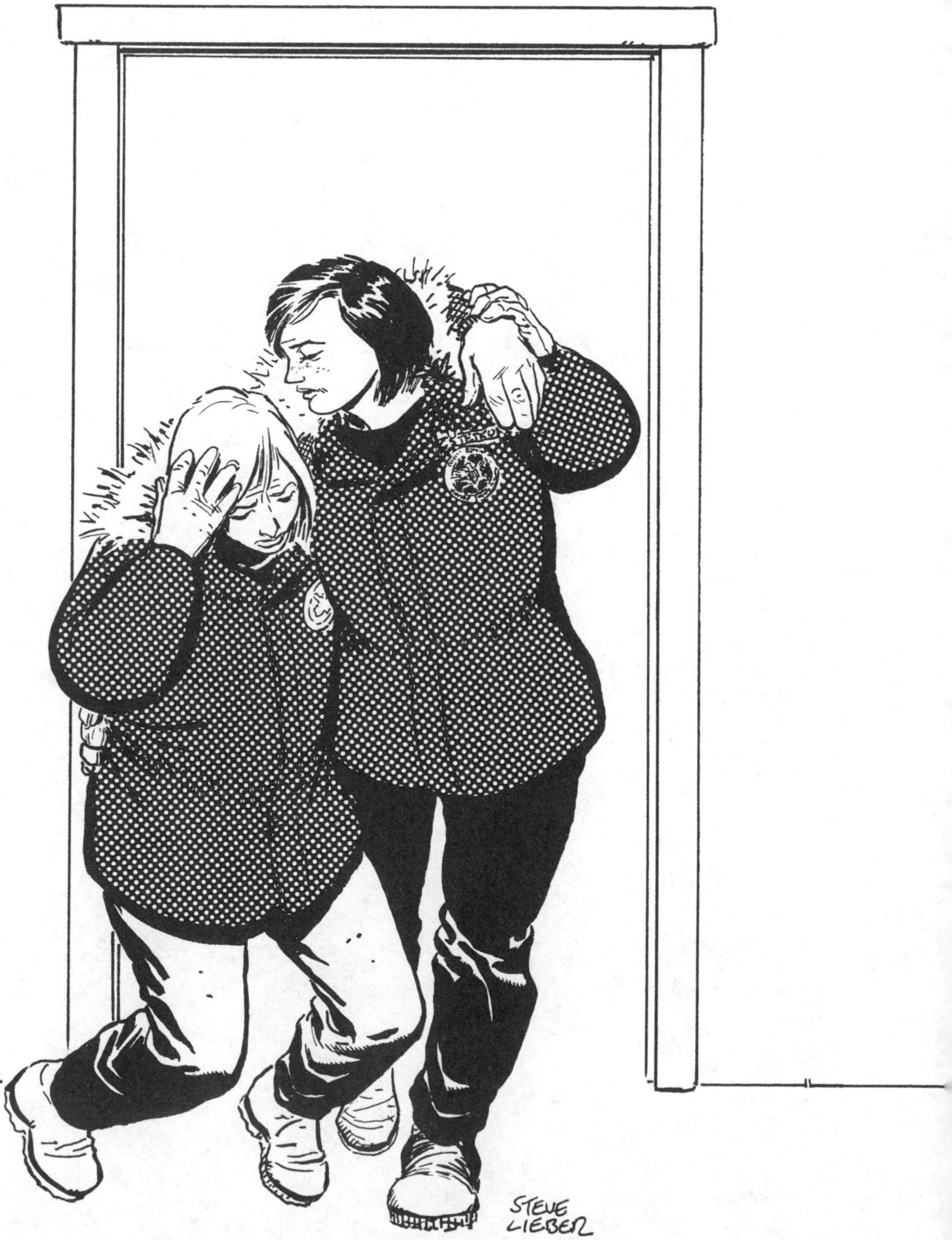
STEVE LIEBER

The knife's made by Earl Emerson...

...gift from an S.A.S. bloke I went with once.

David, his name was.

David's dead now...

...knife still works.

DAMN BITCH!

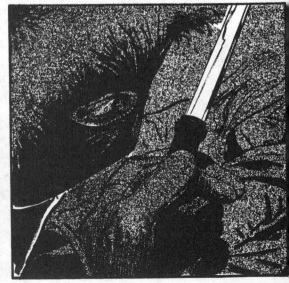

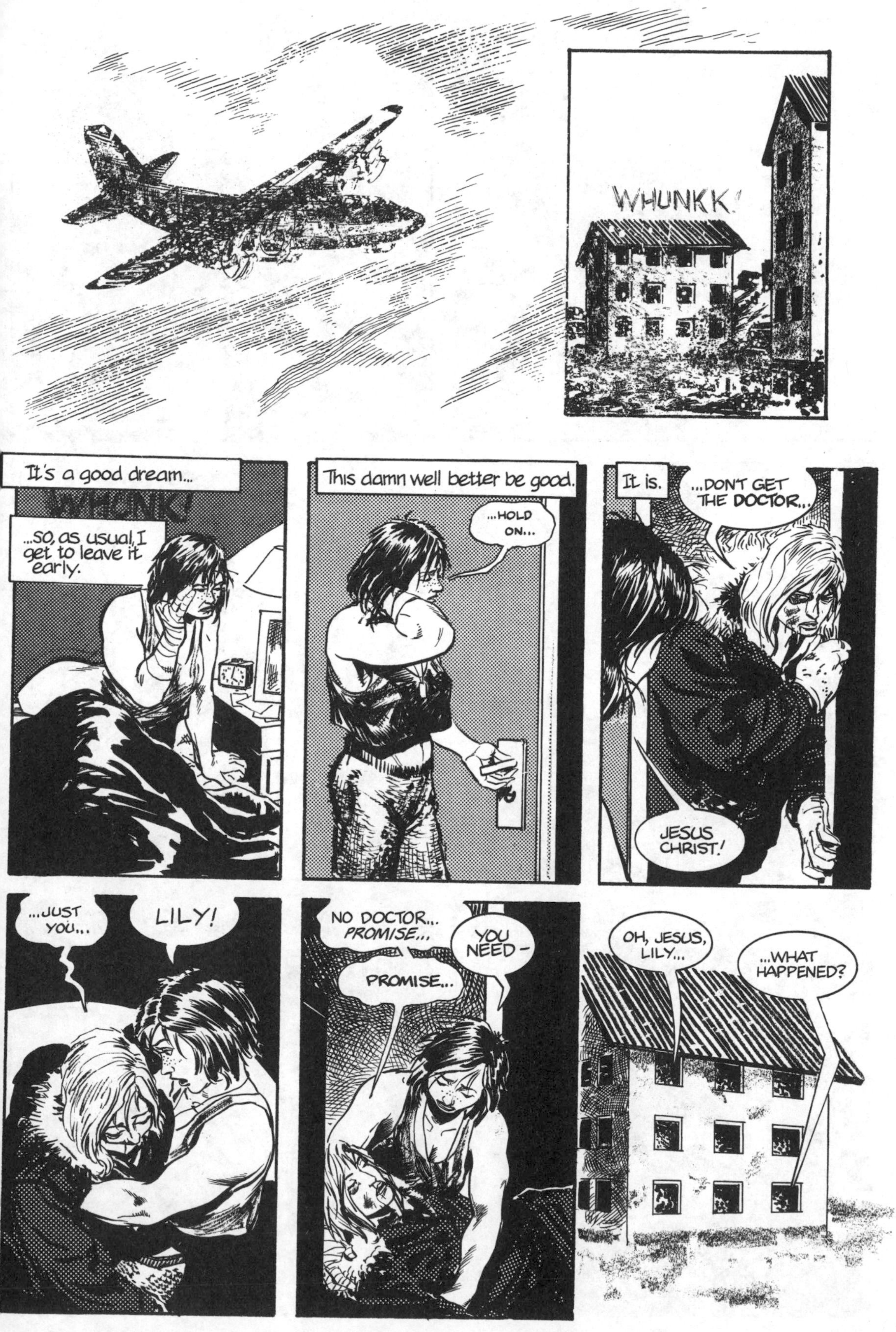
WHUNKK!
It's a good dream...
WHUNK!
...so, as usual, I get to leave it early.
This damn well better be good.
...HOLD ON...
It is.
...DON'T GET THE DOCTOR...
JESUS CHRIST!
...JUST YOU...
LILY!
NO DOCTOR... PROMISE...
PROMISE...
YOU NEED-
OH, JESUS, LILY...
...WHAT HAPPENED?

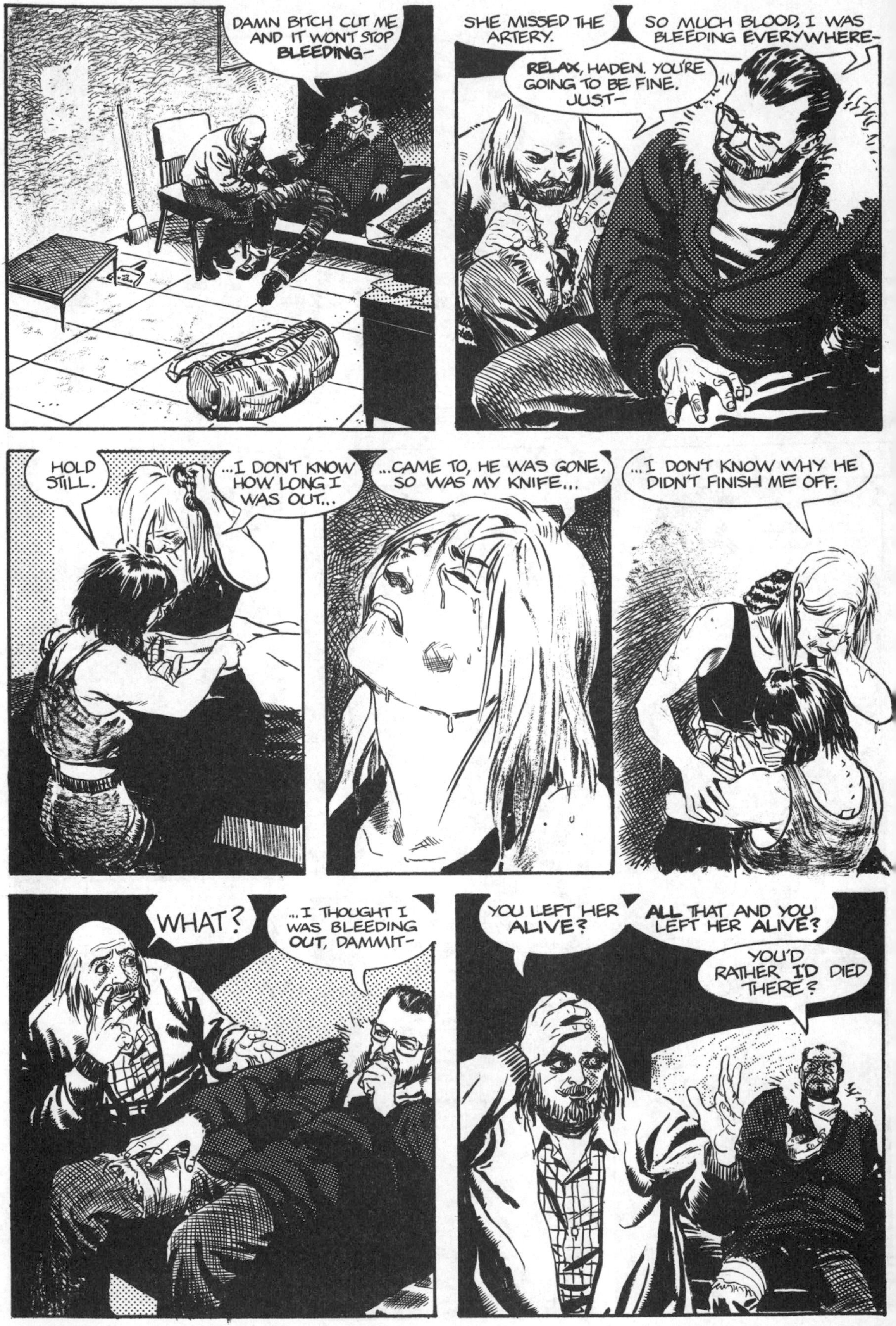
DAMN BITCH CUT ME AND IT WON'T STOP BLEEDING-
SHE MISSED THE ARTERY.
SO MUCH BLOOD, I WAS BLEEDING EVERYWHERE-
RELAX, HADEN. YOU'RE GOING TO BE FINE. JUST-
HOLD STILL.
...I DON'T KNOW HOW LONG I WAS OUT...
...CAME TO, HE WAS GONE, SO WAS MY KNIFE...
...I DON'T KNOW WHY HE DIDN'T FINISH ME OFF.
WHAT?
...I THOUGHT I WAS BLEEDING OUT, DAMMIT-
YOU LEFT HER ALIVE?
ALL THAT AND YOU LEFT HER ALIVE?
YOU'D RATHER I'D DIED THERE?

WHERE ARE WE GOING?

HURRY UP!

DOC? WHERE YOU **TAKIN'** ME?

ALMOST THERE.

GET TO SCOTT BASE, IT'S ONLY TWELVE MILES AWAY...

VMF

..WE FIND YOU A SNOWMOBILE-

I KNOW WHAT YOU'RE TRYING TO DO.

HUH?

WHAT THE HELL ARE YOU TALKING ABOUT?

I **KNOW.** TRYING TO KEEP THE GOLD FOR YOURSELF.

KELLER'S LOCKED AWAY, I'M OUTTA THE WAY, AND YOU...

OLD MAN, I CAN SEE RIGHT THROUGH YOU.

NO-

YOU'LL TELL THE MARSHAL WHERE I WENT, IS **THAT** IT?

HADEN, FOR GOD'S SAKE-

SNIK

BUT MAYBE **I** KILL YOU AND THEN TELL THE MARSHAL, AND SHE'LL THINK **YOU** WERE BEHIND IT ALL?

...DON'T.

GOD.

OH GOD
OH GOD NO
NO NO...

I **SHOULD** BE DEAD.

HAD TO BE HADEN. HE'S A PILOT.

BUT **WHY** ATTACK YOU?

BECAUSE I SAW FURRY AND HIM **WHISPERING** YESTERDAY...

...WHILE **YOU** WERE IN WITH KELLER.

DOESN'T MAKE EITHER OF THEM KELLER'S ACCOMPLICE.

HADEN IS A **PILOT,** CARRIE.

AND FURRY'S A **DOCTOR,** WHAT'S YOUR POINT?

KELLER COULD HAVE HAD **TWO** ACCOMPLICES.

BEG YOUR PARDON?

WE DON'T **KNOW** THIS ATTACK HAS ANYTHING TO DO WITH KELLER.

YOU KNOW WHAT I MEAN.

I'M AFRAID I DON'T

YOU'RE A **FUCKING SPOOK,** LILY. WHY IS A **SPY** FOLLOWING ME AROUND THE ICE?

YOUR ANIMAL MAGNETISM.

CUT THE BULLSHIT, DAMMIT! I KNOW YOU'RE A BRITISH AGENT...

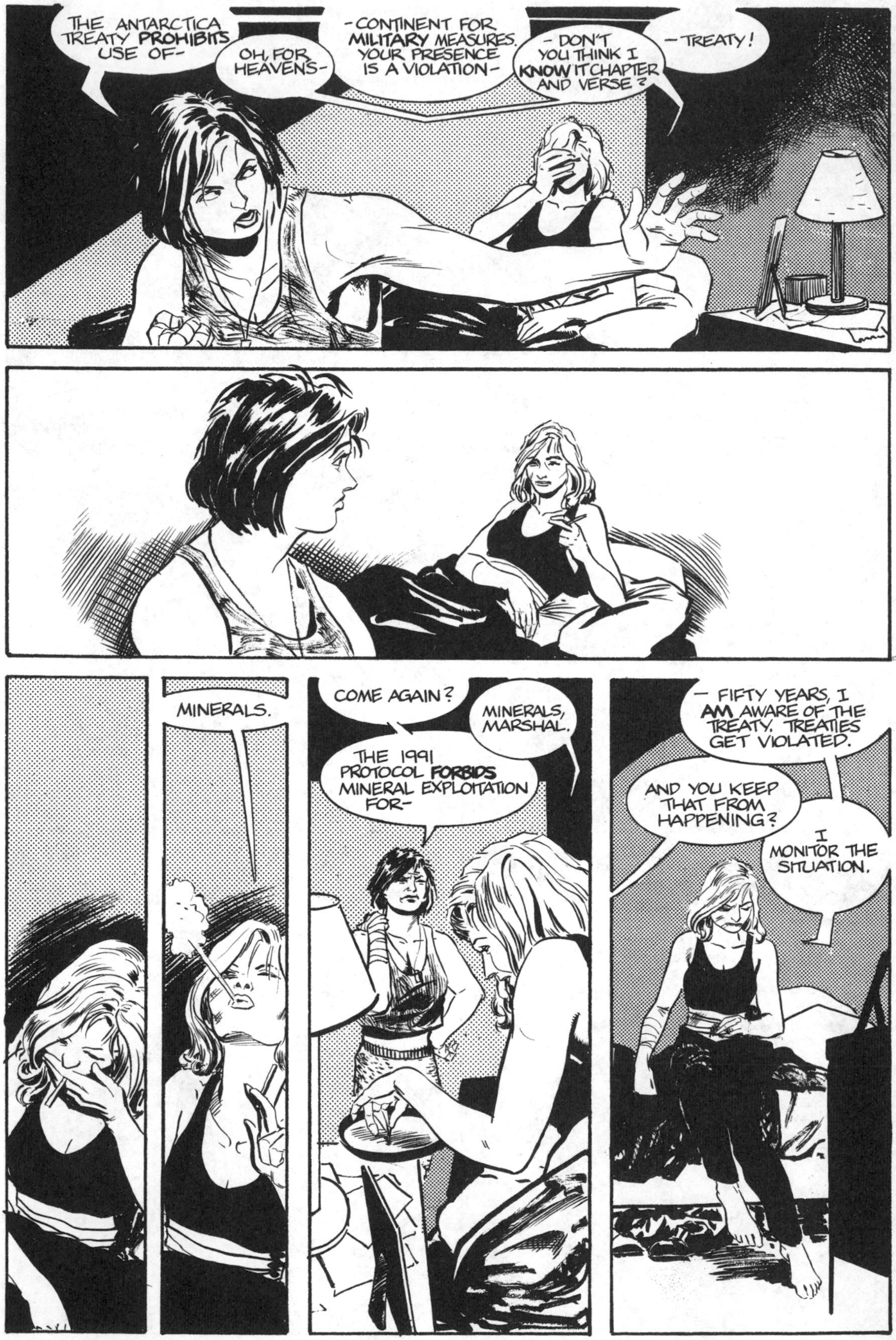
THE ANTARCTICA TREATY PROHIBITS USE OF-
OH, FOR HEAVENS-
-CONTINENT FOR MILITARY MEASURES. YOUR PRESENCE IS A VIOLATION-
- DON'T YOU THINK I KNOW IT CHAPTER AND VERSE?
-TREATY!
MINERALS.
COME AGAIN?
MINERALS, MARSHAL.
THE 1991 PROTOCOL FORBIDS MINERAL EXPLOITATION FOR-
- FIFTY YEARS, I AM AWARE OF THE TREATY. TREATIES GET VIOLATED.
AND YOU KEEP THAT FROM HAPPENING?
I MONITOR THE SITUATION.

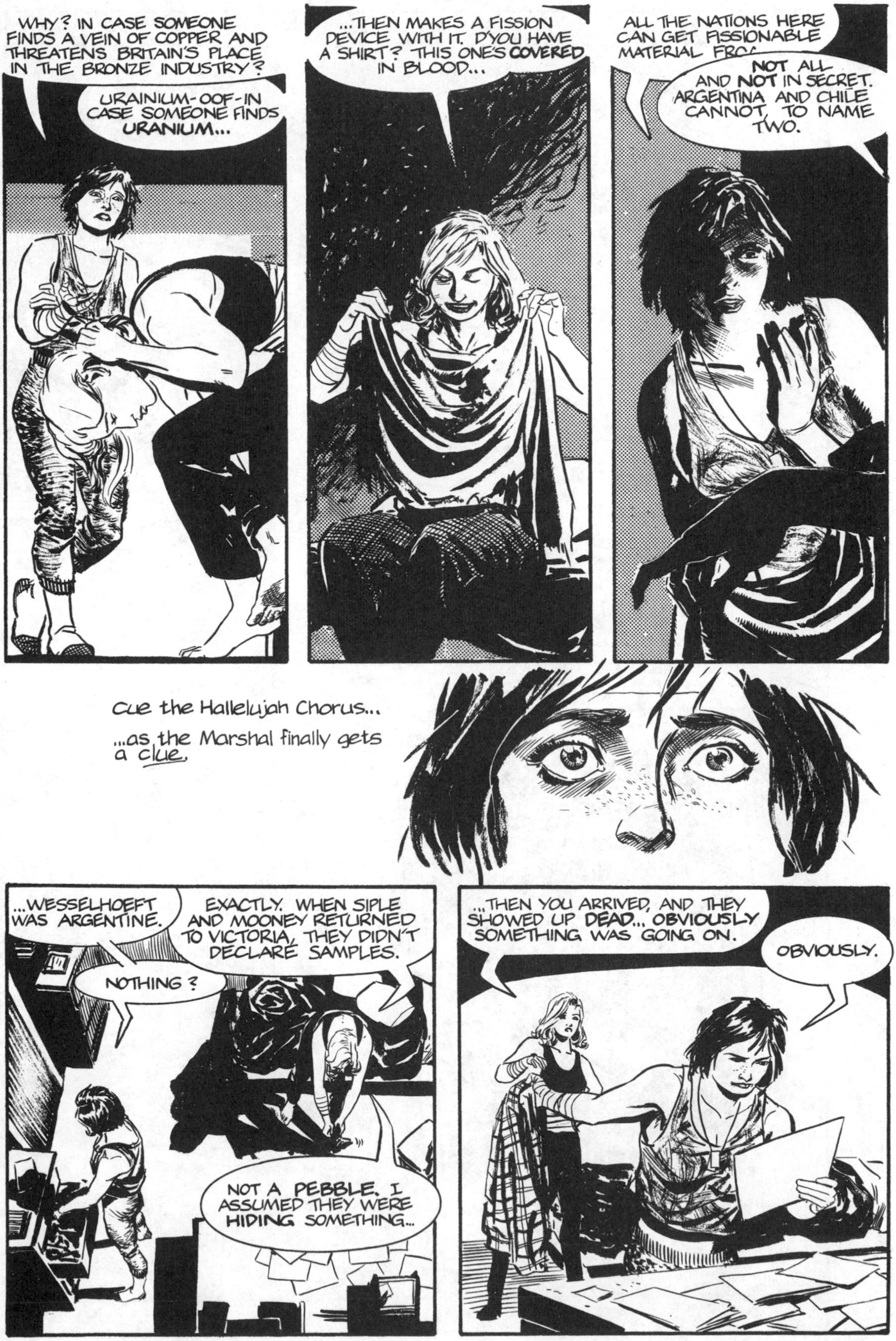
WHY? IN CASE SOMEONE FINDS A VEIN OF COPPER AND THREATENS BRITAIN'S PLACE IN THE BRONZE INDUSTRY?
URAINIUM-OOF-IN CASE SOMEONE FINDS URANIUM...
...THEN MAKES A FISSION DEVICE WITH IT. D'YOU HAVE A SHIRT? THIS ONE'S COVERED IN BLOOD...
ALL THE NATIONS HERE CAN GET FISSIONABLE MATERIAL FRO
NOT ALL AND NOT IN SECRET. ARGENTINA AND CHILE CANNOT, TO NAME TWO.
Cue the Hallelujah Chorus...
...as the Marshal finally gets a clue.
...WESSELHOEFT WAS ARGENTINE.
EXACTLY. WHEN SIPLE AND MOONEY RETURNED TO VICTORIA, THEY DIDN'T DECLARE SAMPLES.
NOTHING?
NOT A PEBBLE. I ASSUMED THEY WERE HIDING SOMETHING...
...THEN YOU ARRIVED, AND THEY SHOWED UP DEAD... OBVIOUSLY SOMETHING WAS GOING ON.
OBVIOUSLY.

THERE'S NO URANIUM.

I KNOW.

THIS IS ABOUT **GREED.** THIS IS ABOUT GETTING THE GOLD OFF THE ICE.

HADEN. HE'S A **PILOT.** FLIES FOR THE KIWIS.

KELLER WAS GOING TO THE US. HE WOULDN'T WANT HADEN HOLDING THE GOLD IN AUSTRALIA.

WE SHOULD GRAB HADEN THEN.

LET ME GET DRESSED...

...THIS IS A PAIN WHEN YOU ONLY HAVE ONE GOOD HAND.

I WOULD IMAGINE.

WHAT WAS HIS NAME?

MAL. MALCOLM. HE WAS AN ATTORNEY. A U.S. ATTORNEY...

HOW'D HE DIE?

IF YOU DON'T MIND MY ASKING, OF COURSE

...CANCER, RIGHT AFTER WE MARRIED...

THIS WAS AFTER I'D BEEN SUSPENDED FOR THE PRICE THING— DAMMIT!—

HERE.

CHEMO MADE HIM SO WEAK...DIED BEFORE OUR FIRST ANNIVERSARY...

LET ME GET THAT.

ME GET THAT...

I LOVE YOU, MARSHAL.

LOVE YOU, TOO, COUNSELOR.

LET'S GO KICK HADEN'S ASS.

The clock's ticking down, now.
McEwan or one of his cronies is on that flight...

...here to transport the prisoner back to the world.

The last flight out of town.

HOWDY, MARSHAL, HERE TO SAY **GOODBYE?**

YOU'RE ON THAT FLIGHT?

BET YOUR CUTE ASS. WHAT HAP—

DON'T ASK. SEEN HADEN?

DURING BAG-DRAG THIS MORNING GOING SOMEWHERE WITH DOC.

FURRY?

YEAH. LOOKED LIKE THEY WERE HURRYING. COURSE THAT MIGHT'VE BEEN THE **COLD.**

WHICH WAY?

TOWARDS VMF, I THINK. WHY?

IF HADEN GRABBED A VEHICLE, HE'S HEADED FOR SCOTT—

YOU GO.

That's **it**

TAKE THE LOO.

WHERE ARE YOU HEADED?

Let me be wrong.

**Please** let me be wrong.

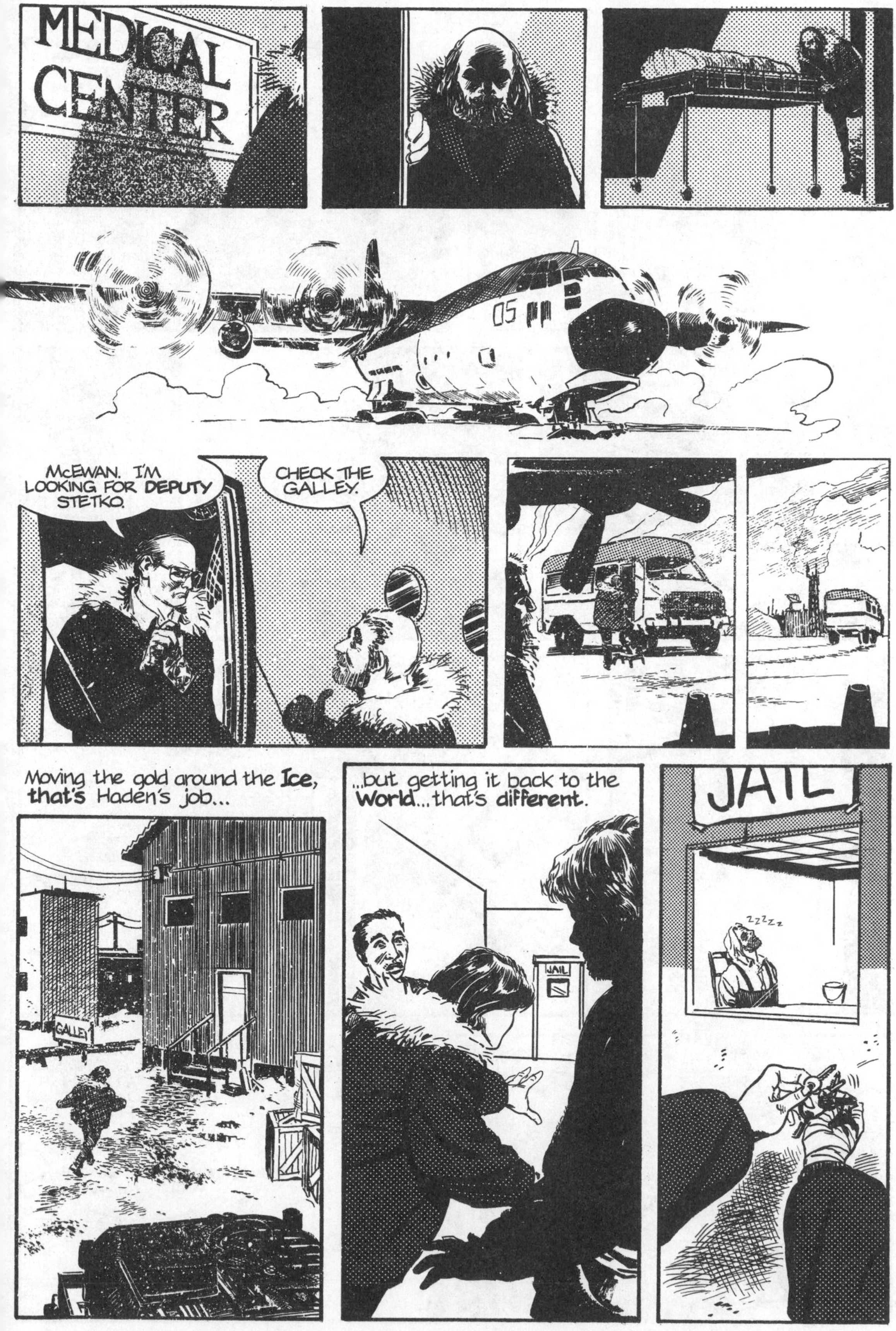
MEDICAL CENTER
McEWAN. I'M LOOKING FOR DEPUTY STETKO.
CHECK THE GALLEY.
Moving the gold around the Ice, that's Haden's job...
...but getting it back to the World... that's different.
GALLEY
JAIL
JAIL
ZZZZZ

...CAN'T BELIEVE THAT HADEN IS INVOLVED WITH ANY OF THIS. HE'S NOT LIKE THAT.

YOU'RE SO CERTAIN.

HE'S A... DRINKING... BUDDY...

SON OF A BITCH!

LIEUTENANT?

I TOLD HIM **EVERYTHING**...**WHERE** CARRIE WENT, **WHO** SHE TALKED TO... WE SHOULD **WARN** HER.

NO NEED.

THAT'S **FIVE**.

..."WHA?"...

NEVER MIND.

I WANT TO KNOW, ALEX

FUCKING BLOW ME, CUN-

WHO ELSE, ALEX? HADEN AND **WHO ELSE?**

〈gurk〉 ...CHOKING ME...

...CAN'T 〈ock〉 DO THIS...

WHO'S GOING TO **STOP** ME? YOU?

HADEN COULDN'T FLY THE GOLD OUT HIMSELF— **WEIGHS** TOO MUCH. IT HAD TO GO OUT ON A **BIG** PLANE...

A HERC, MAYBE, LIKE THE ONE THAT JUST **LANDED** AT WILLY FIELD.

BUT HOW WERE YOU GOING TO GET IT ON BOARD?

..AHK?..

HOW, ALEX?

...CAN'T... BREATHE...

I KNOW.

HOW, ALEX?

...TELL... YOU...

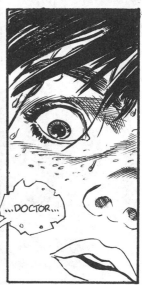

...DOCTOR...

FURRY...

FURRY... WHY?

DEPUTY! WHAT THE FU—

SIR, YOUR PRISONER IS READY FOR TRANSPORT.

AND WHERE THE HELL ARE YOU GOING?

...UNFINISHED BUSINESS.

DELFY WILL GIVE YOU A HAND.

ZIPPPRRRRRRRR

WONDERED WHEN YOU'D GET HERE.

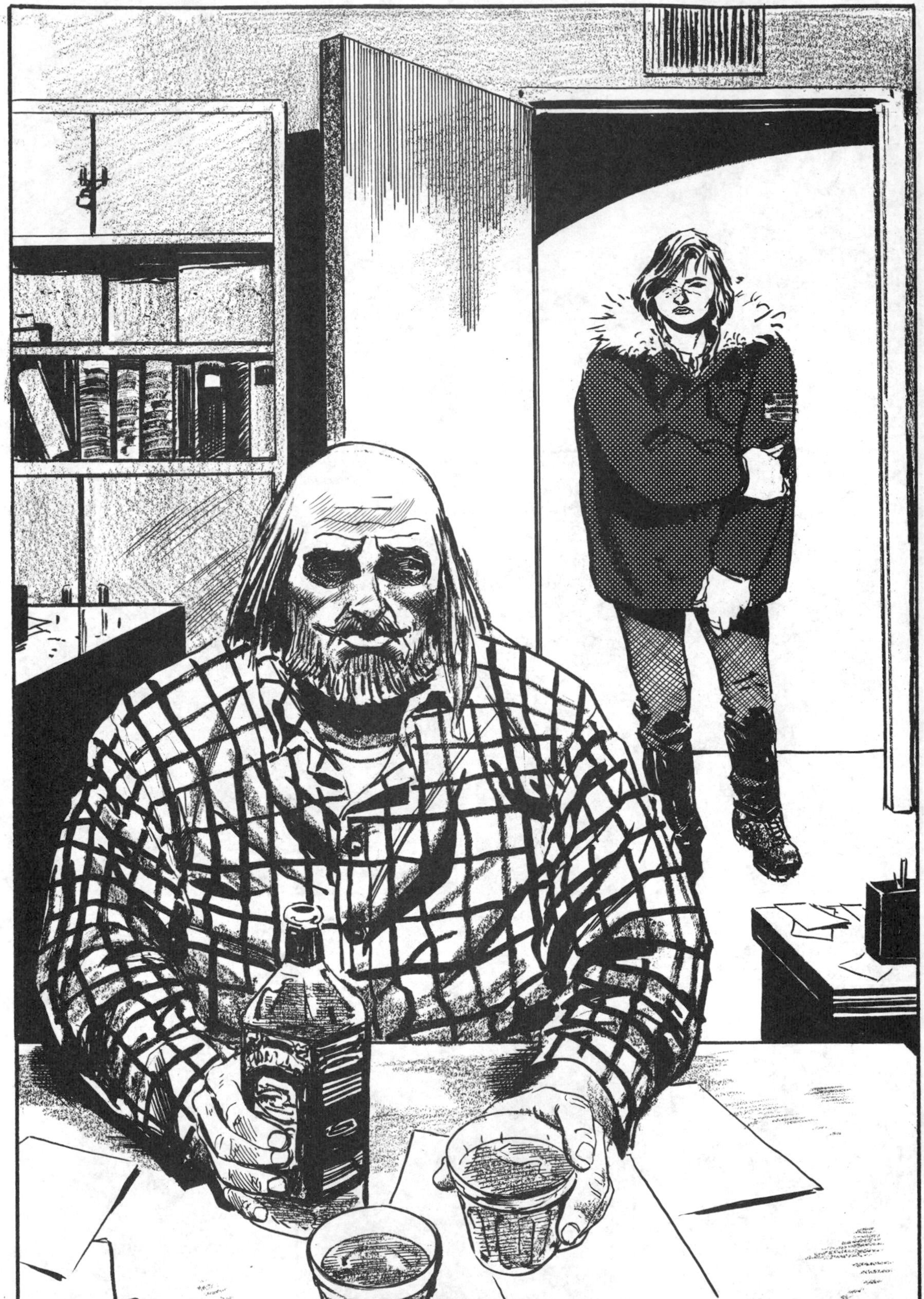

ONE LAST DRINK? FOR OLD TIME'S SAKE?

FOR OLD TIME'S SAKE, CARRIE?

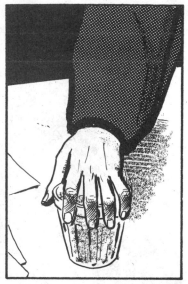

CHEERS.

YOU'VE GOT THE RIGHT TO REMAIN SILENT, HERE, FURRY.

DID KELLER FINALLY TALK, OR DID YOU FIND HADEN'S BODY?

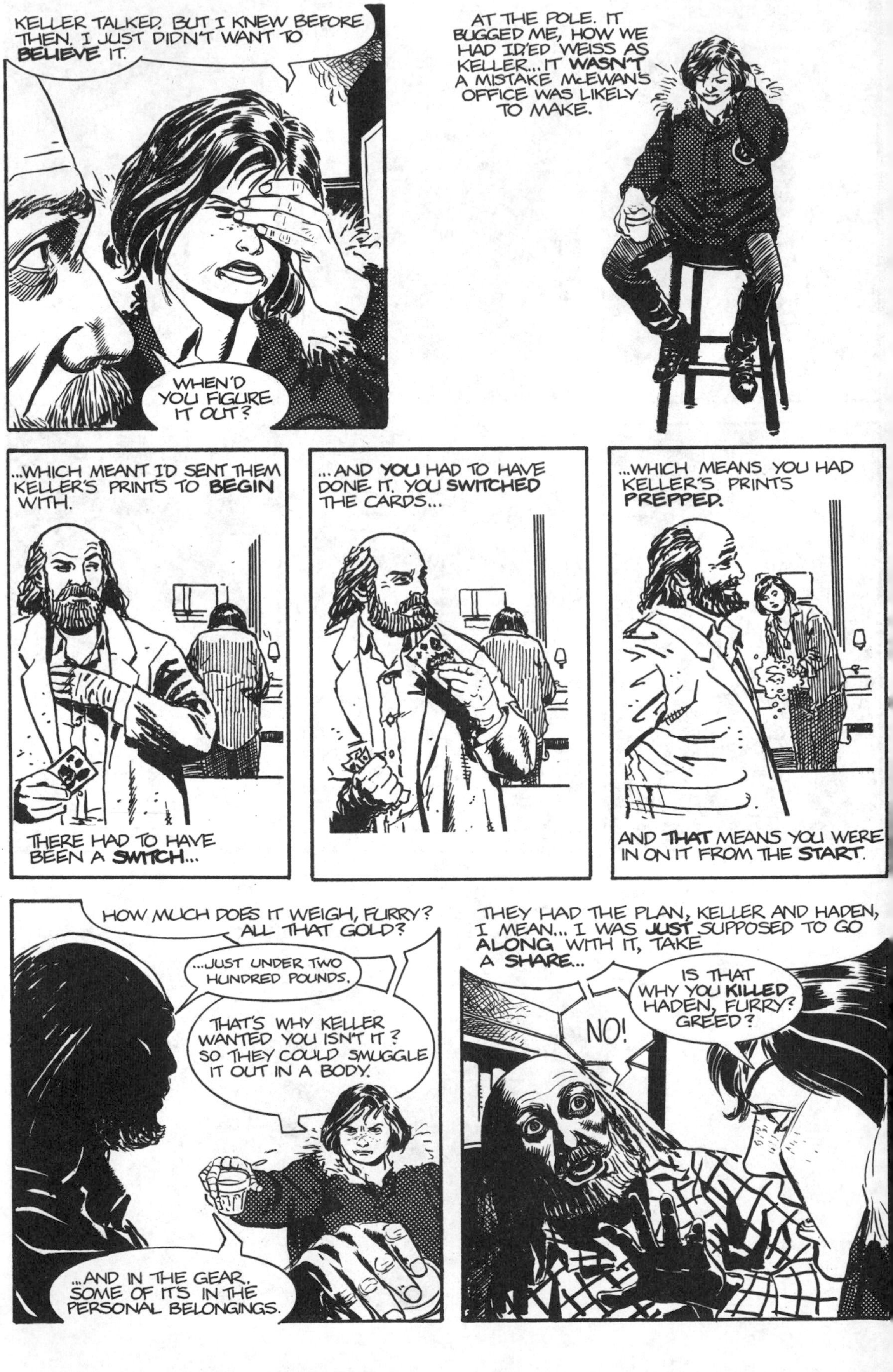
KELLER TALKED. BUT I KNEW BEFORE THEN. I JUST DIDN'T WANT TO **BELIEVE** IT.
WHEN'D YOU FIGURE IT OUT?
AT THE POLE. IT BUGGED ME, HOW WE HAD ID'ED WEISS AS KELLER... IT **WASN'T** A MISTAKE McEWAN'S OFFICE WAS LIKELY TO MAKE.
...WHICH MEANT I'D SENT THEM KELLER'S PRINTS TO **BEGIN** WITH.
THERE HAD TO HAVE BEEN A **SWITCH**...
...AND **YOU** HAD TO HAVE DONE IT. YOU **SWITCHED** THE CARDS...
...WHICH MEANS YOU HAD KELLER'S PRINTS **PREPPED**.
AND **THAT** MEANS YOU WERE IN ON IT FROM THE **START**.
HOW MUCH DOES IT WEIGH, FURRY? ALL THAT GOLD?
...JUST UNDER TWO HUNDRED POUNDS.
THAT'S WHY KELLER WANTED YOU ISN'T IT? SO THEY COULD SMUGGLE IT OUT IN A BODY.
...AND IN THE GEAR. SOME OF IT'S IN THE PERSONAL BELONGINGS.
THEY HAD THE PLAN, KELLER AND HADEN, I MEAN... I WAS **JUST** SUPPOSED TO GO **ALONG** WITH IT, TAKE A **SHARE**...
IS THAT WHY YOU **KILLED** HADEN, FURRY? GREED?
NO!

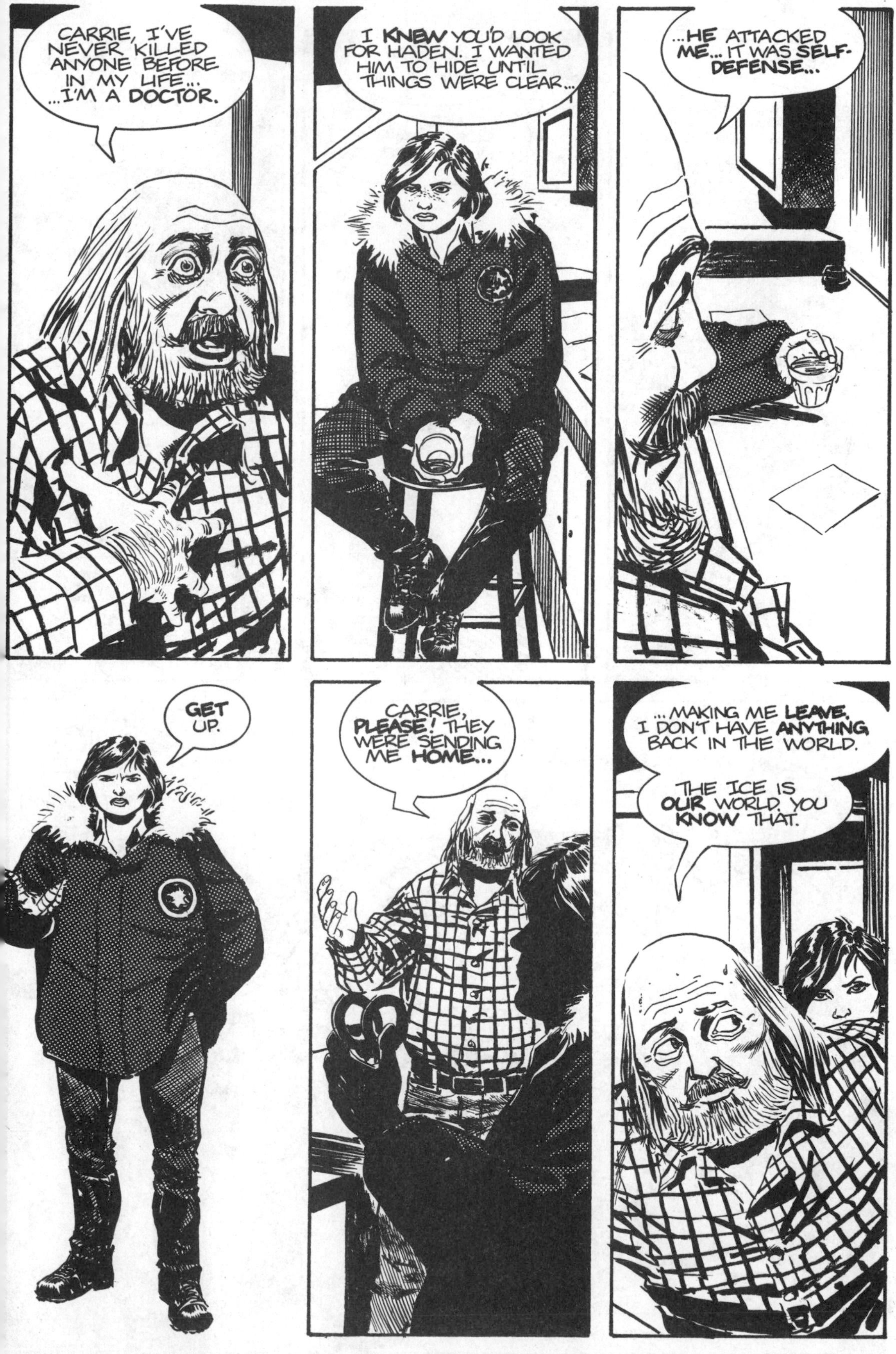
CARRIE, I'VE NEVER KILLED ANYONE BEFORE IN MY LIFE... ...I'M A DOCTOR.
I KNEW YOU'D LOOK FOR HADEN. I WANTED HIM TO HIDE UNTIL THINGS WERE CLEAR...
...HE ATTACKED ME... IT WAS SELF-DEFENSE...
GET UP.
CARRIE, PLEASE! THEY WERE SENDING ME HOME...
...MAKING ME LEAVE. I DON'T HAVE ANYTHING BACK IN THE WORLD.
THE ICE IS OUR WORLD. YOU KNOW THAT.

"The Ice is our world...

...you're just like me..."

Maybe

Or maybe I'm **thawing**

It's the **gold** that McEwan latches onto. **Greed**, that's easy for him to understand...

...I don't bother trying to explain that there's **more** to it than that...

...**much** more...

It's the **Ice**, after all...

...it **changes** you...

...and either you **get** it, or you **don't**.

Winter

Eight months of dark and cold.

It'll be all right.

I'll stay warm.

GREG RUCKA +
STEVE LIEBER
1995

# AFTERWORD

I was at a con in Portland, hanging with the Oni crew. At that point, I'm there feeling like a fraud—I mean, I'm sitting behind the Oni table like I deserve to be there or some such, and the truth of the matter is, I've got nothing to show for it. Just this idea, this story about a female Federal Marshal in Antarctica and some dead guys. An idea that, for some reason, Joe Nozemack and Bob Schreck like enough to want to publish. I've even written a script of the first issue...but that's not really an attention grabber when you're sitting behind a table at a convention.

Let's face it, the comic is nothing without the art.

And that's been the problem—who's going to draw this insanity? And it is insanity, because the requirements here are strict—we need an artist who can draw cold and who can do it in black-and-white. We need an artist who can draw people, not caricatures. We need an artist who can research, who can make it all look, if not real, at least realistic. Most importantly, we need an artist who can draw women. Not Bad Girls, not Pin-Ups, not Top-Heavy Genetic Aberrations, but women.

Schreck points me to this table, where a lone artist is doing sketches and basically trying to make a living. Schreck gives me a shove.

"Take a look at his stuff," Bob says. "Let me know what you think."

If you don't know Schreck, when he gives you a shove, you go. Whether you want to or not, you go.

I go.

Five minutes later and I'm back, now holding three prints signed by Steve Lieber. Paid good money for those—they're on my wall as I type this.

"Well?" asks Bob.

"Hell, yeah," I say.

One month later, and I'm getting a phone call from Lieber at midnight, and he's telling me to get offline, dammit, he wants to fax me some stuff. I take the first sheet as it comes out and my jaw drops, because I'm looking at Carrie Stetko. And he's nailed it, I mean, this is what's been in my head the whole damn time.

Well, except for the hair, but Steve fixes that.

And then it's perfect.

And I think, whoa...this is going to be cool. I think, this might actually work.

I still think it's cool. I still think it worked.

Hopefully, you do, too.

GREG RUCKA
Portland
March, 1999

# OTHER BOOKS BY GREG RUCKA

## FROM ONI PRESS

### WHITEOUT: MELT

by Greg Rucka & Steve Lieber
128 pages, black-and-white interiors
$11.95 US, $17.95 CAN
ISBN 1-929998-03-1

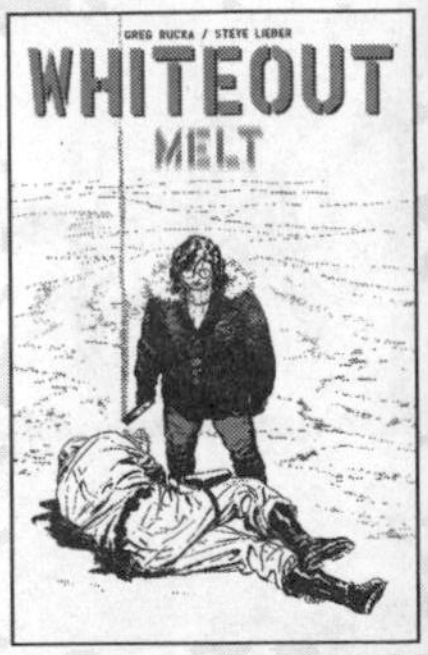
GREG RUCKA / STEVE LIEBER
WHITEOUT
MELT

## THE ATTICUS KODIAK NOVELS FROM BANTAM BOOKS

### KEEPER

$5.99 US, $7.99 CAN
ISBN 0-553-57428-0

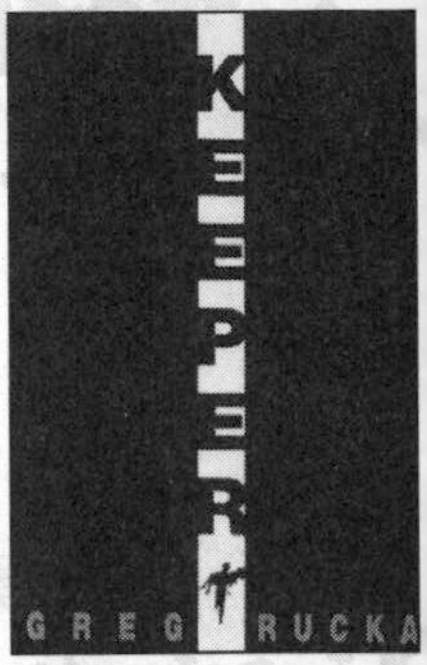
KEEPER
GREG RUCKA

### FINDER

$5.99 US, $7.99 CAN
ISBN 0-553-57429-9

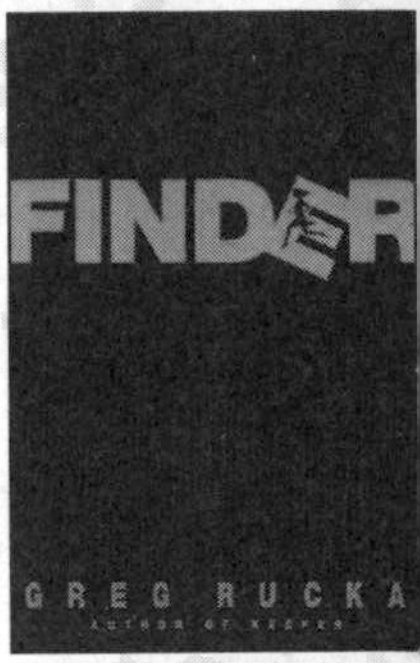
FINDER
GREG RUCKA

### SMOKER

$5.99 US, $7.99 CAN
ISBN 0-553-57829-4

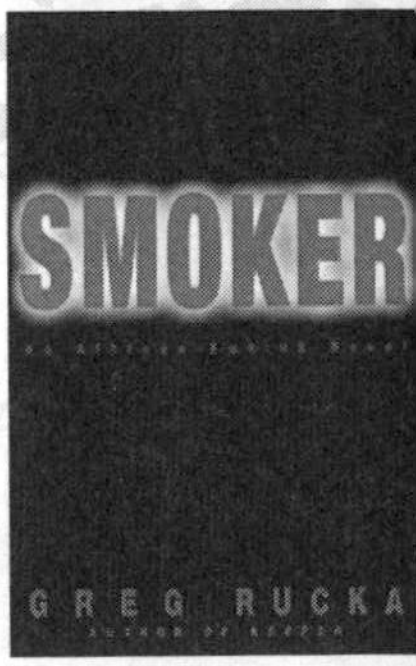
SMOKER
GREG RUCKA

### SHOOTING AT MIDNIGHT

hardcover edition
$23.95 US, $34.95 CAN
ISBN 0-553-10720-8

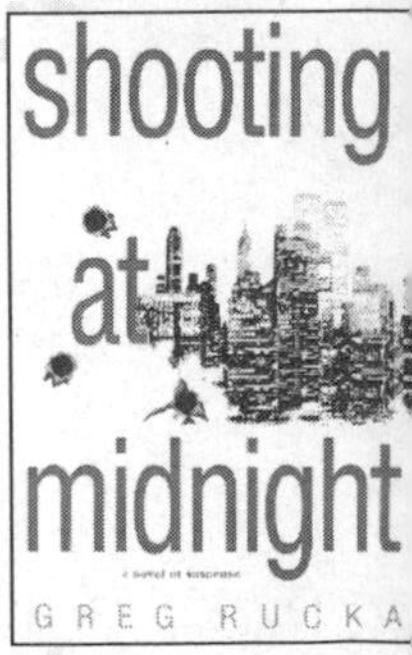
shooting
at
midnight
GREG RUCKA

Available at finer bookstores everywhere.